one hundred poets, one poem each

Translations from the Asian Classics

Translations from the Asian Classics

EDITORIAL BOARD

WM. THEODORE DE BARY, CHAIR
PAUL ANDERER
IRENE BLOOM
DONALD KEENE
GEORGE A. SALIBA
HARUO SHIRANE
WEI SHANG
BURTON WATSON

One Hundred Poets, One Poem Each

A Translation of the Ogura Hyakunin Isshu

PETER McMILLAN

Foreword by Donald Keene

Columbia University Press New York

Columbia University Press
Publishers Since 1893
New York   Chichester, West Sussex

Copyright © 2008 Columbia University Press
All rights reserved

Library of Congress Cataloging-in-Publication Data
Ogura hyakunin isshu. English & Japanese.
One hundred poets, one poem each : a translation of the Ogura hyakunin isshu / by
    Peter McMillan ; foreword by Donald Keene.
        p.   cm. — (Translations from the Asian classics)
    Includes bibliographical references.
    English and Japanese.
    ISBN 978-0-231-14398-1 (cloth : alk. paper)
    1. Waka—Translations into English.   2. Japanese poetry—To 1600—Translations
        into English.   I. McMillan, Peter.   II. Title.   III. Series.
PL758.5.O4A3   2008
895.6'1008—dc22
                                                                2007013824

∞

Columbia University Press books are printed on permanent and durable acid-free paper.
This book was printed on paper with recycled content.
Printed in the United States of America
c 10 9 8 7 6 5 4 3 2

References to Internet Web sites (URLs) were accurate at the time of writing. Neither the author nor Columbia University Press is responsible for URLs that may have expired or changed since the manuscript was prepared.

FOR MY MOTHER AND FATHER

CONTENTS

Foreword by Donald Keene ix

Acknowledgments xv

Introduction xix

The Poems 1

*Appendix: The Colors of the Flower: Poem 9 as an Example of Code Language
and Multiplicity of Meanings in* Waka 105

Afterword by Eileen Kato 111

Notes on the Poems 115

Notes on the Poets 131

Waka *and Romanized Transliteration of* Waka 155

Glossary 177

Bibliography 179

Illustration Credits 183

FOREWORD

The first Japanese work of literature to be translated into English was the *Ogura Hyakunin Isshu* (or *Hyakunin Isshu*). The translator was identified only as "a Medical Officer of the Royal Navy," but later versions of the same translation revealed he was Frederick Victor Dickins (1835–1915). Dickins was sent to East Asia as a young officer, and from 1863 onward he served as medical officer at the British legation in Yokohama. An early account of Dickins says that he studied Japanese "out of personal desire." His first translation of *Hyakunin Isshu* appeared in the March 1865 issue of the *Chinese and Japanese Repository*.

Dickins learned Japanese amazingly well, considering the difficulties: Not only were there no suitable textbooks for beginners in Japanese, but the text on which he based his translation was printed in *hentaigana*, a perversely difficult script. His second version of *Hyakunin Isshu* (published in London in 1866) was an extensive revision of the first, reflecting an improved knowledge of Japanese. The translations are occasionally felicitous, but they are marred by a perceived necessity to render it in rhyme felt by Dickins (and others of the day). It is cruel to Dickins to quote his translations from early in his study of Japanese poetry, at a time when no one else was making translations. Presenting them, however, reveals, more clearly than any explanation, both the difficulties that he experienced in understanding the original poems and the follies that were committed in the name of rhyme. The following are two translations by Dickins of the *Hyakunin Isshu* poem attributed to Semimaru, the fourth son of the Emperor Daigo (r. 897–930):

VERSION 1:

These multitudes before me
Pass by;—they come, they go;—
And tho' I strive full surely
To recognize friend or foe,
As ignorant as the barrier-gate,
Of mountain-path, my wretched fate.

VERSION 2:

Some hence towards the city haste,
Some from the city here speed by,
Here friends and strangers meet and part,
With kindly glance and careless eye:
Apt is the name it seems to me,
Ausaka gate, men give to thee.

William N. Porter's translations, published in 1909, are in the same "poetic" vein:

The stranger who has traveled far,
The friend with welcome smile,
All sorts of men who come and go
Meet at this mountain stile,—
They meet and rest awhile.

Japanese scholars who translated the *Hyakunin Isshu* into English were equally susceptible to the allure of rhyme, as this 1956 version by H. H. Honda suggests:

> Lo, at this barrier people greet,
> Those leaving home, and those who hope
> Home to return; so it is meet
> To call the barrier Trysting Slope.

It is hard to believe that these are all translations of the same poem. Apart from the out-and-out mistakes, their worst feature is the padding to which the translations resorted in order to achieve rhyme, against all reason. My more literal version of the same poem, from 1953, reads:

> This is the Barrier
> Where people come and people go
> Exchanging farewells;
> For friends and strangers alike
> This is Meeting Barrier.

The third line in my translation does not correspond to anything in the original. Why did I include it? Probably because I wanted to maintain, as closely as I could, the form of the original, a poem written in lines of 5, 7, 5, 7, and 7 syllables. It seemed important to maintain this form, employed by Japanese with little variation for more than a thousand years.

At first glance, therefore, I was rather prejudiced against Peter McMillan's new translation because of the freedom that he took with the form. But his version of the same poem by Semimaru changed my mind completely:

> So this is the place!
> The crowds,
> coming,
> going,
> meeting,
> parting;
> friends
> strangers
> known
> unknown—
> Osaka Barrier.

As I read this translation, I came to believe that it was the most successful one ever rendered of the poem. McMillan's daring in expanding to eleven lines the five of the original had helped to create an exciting English poem. The translation is not only effective but accurate, even to the exclamation in the first line that earlier translators omitted; and the repetition of words ending in "-ing" convey the rhythm of the original.

Sometimes in McMillan's translations the choice of one word brings out the implications of the original. I particularly liked his rendition of the poem by the Emperor Sutoku (r. 1123–1141):

> Like water
> rushing down
> the river rapids
> we may be parted
> by a rock,
> but in the end
> we will be one again.

No subject is provided in the Japanese original for the predicates "may be parted" or "will be one again." Most earlier versions had translated the subject as "it"—meaning it (the water), though parted by a rock in the river, comes together again when past the rock. This is indeed the surface meaning, but surely the poet intended to make more than a simple observation of a scene. Even though Sutoku did not say "we," he must have expected readers to understand that when writing of the rushing river he was referring to himself. McMillan's use of "we" makes his translation of the poem haunting.

The great poet Fujiwara Teika (1162–1241), the compiler of *One Hundred Poets, One Poem Each*, did not reveal the reasons for his choice of poems. The poems range from those from the eighth-century anthology *Man'yōshū* to those of the thirteenth century, including one by Teika himself. Some are marked by complex verbal ingenuity that resulted from the poets' attempt to make richer the bare thirty-one syllables at their command, but others, like the following by Fun'ya no Asayasu, a poet of the tenth century, have an appealing simplicity in McMillan's translation:

> When the wind gusts
> over the Autumn fields
> the glistening white dewdrops
> lie strewn about
> like scattered pearls.

A few of the poems are anonymous, but the known authors were members of the Japanese court. This undoubtedly accounts for the elegance in the diction, the absence of words or themes that might be thought crude. The popularity of the collection, which persists to this day in Japan, profoundly affected the composition of poetry until well into the nineteenth century, restricting the subjects worthy of poetic composition but aiming at perfection in every detail.

Peter McMillan's translation of the *Ogura Hyakunin Isshu* has restored the importance and beauty of a collection of poetry too often dismissed as merely "pretty." The poems Fujiwara Teika selected possess great beauty, but they move us also in the unmistakable feeling that flows in a poem such as one by the Emperor Kōkō (r. 884–887), which in McMillan's version reads:

> For you,
> I went out to the fields
> to pick the first Spring greens—
> all the while on my sleeves
> a light snow falling.

This is by far the best translation of the *Ogura Hyakunin Isshu* to date.

Donald Keene

ACKNOWLEDGMENTS

I acquired my limited knowledge of classical Japanese during a two-year sabbatical at Princeton, Columbia, and Oxford universities from 1996 to 1998. My deepest thanks go to Dr. Hiroharu and Mrs. Yasuko Matsuda of Kyōrin University and the Japanese Ministry of Education for making this sabbatical possible. More recently, Kyōrin University has generously provided a grant to support this volume, for which I express my grateful acknowledgment.

I also thank my principal adviser during my sabbatical, Professor Martin Collcutt of Princeton, to whom I owe a great deal. Professor Henry Smith of Columbia University and Professor James McMullen of Oxford University also helped me in many ways. At Columbia I had the good fortune to study with Professor Donald Keene. Later, he read over this translation in great detail, making many suggestions for improving it. He also kindly agreed to write the foreword. I would be honored if this translation were seen in part as a tribute to the tradition of excellence in Japanese translation that he has established both as a translator and as a teacher. I extend my gratitude as well to David Lurie, Michael Watson, Barbara Ford, Christine Guth, Hisashi Yamada, Toshiko Takaezu,

Yuriko Kuchiki, Neil Gross, Kio Lippit, Anna Suh Hongkyung, and many others who offered me both friendship and encouragement during my time at Columbia and Princeton.

During my sabbatical, I also studied art history. Since returning to Japan both poetry and art have been my main interests. The *Ogura Hyakunin Isshu* brings together both of these domains, which are my principal interests in it. I specialize in contemporary art and poetry and, like Teika, I am interested in contemporary re-inventions of the great art of the past, both Western and Asian. Instead of becoming an art historian, however, I established an art gallery (www.mcmillanart.com) and began to paint. Since that time I have been greatly indebted to Takashi Yamamoto and his son, Yuto, and Masami Tomura and his sons, Rikiya and Takumi, my guides in the art world.

Several people reviewed these translations and made valuable suggestions. I thank Moira Prior, Colm Rowan, Karen Weir-Jimerson, and Moynagh Sullivan. I also thank Minoru and Shigeko Higuchi, Haruyoshi Takeuchi, Toshifumi and Hiroko Saimon, Kei Morishita, Sanae Matsuo, Ken Harada, JoAnn Parochetti, and Takao Akai for their encouragement. The first few poems in this translation benefited from my work with Kikuo Tōyama, whose delicate sensibility helped me to understand their complexity and beauty. In addition, I am indebted to Kazuya Numazawa, whose tireless work as my assistant for three years left me enough time to devote to translation, and to my present assistant, Tōru Aoyama. More recently, Brendan Scannell, Ireland's ambassador to Japan, and his wife, Margaret, have been very supportive. I am also grateful to Toshi Takagishi, Kaishū Takei, Kiyoko Takagi, John Carpenter, Junichi Takeuchi, Monika Dix, Roselee Bundy, and Alexander Vovin. Thanks are due to Hideji Ōyagi, the National Institute of Japanese Literature, the Gifu City Public Library, the Osaka City University Media Center, the Gotoh Museum, and Shiguretei, the Reizei Family Archive, for permission to reproduce various images. Calligraphy accompanying each poem is in the hand of Abbot Genchin and was composed in 1660 (Manji 3) in the fifth month and is reproduced with the kind permission of Osaka City University, Media Center. The line drawings of the one hundred poets by Kuwagata Keisai date from the nineteenth century and are reproduced with the kind permission of the Gifu City Public Library. The other credits are provided under each illustration.

I also acknowledge the guidance and help of the two anonymous readers, editorial board members, and staff of Columbia University Press, especially Jennifer Crewe, and Chang Jae Lee. I also thank my copy editor, Debra E. Soled, for her extremely thorough editing. Scott Spears also read over the manuscript several times, and it is greatly improved because of his many corrections and suggestions. Thanks also go to Yukiko Hirota for her excellent photographs of the card game.

My mother is a writer; from her, I gained a love of writing and literature. My father is an art dealer; from him, I gained a love of art. I hope that this work is the beginning of a tribute to the interests I inherited from both of them and, while taking responsibility for all its shortcomings, I humbly dedicate this translation to them.

I completed most of the work while in Lake Yamanaka, which was introduced to me by the late Sachiko Tanabe, a lady of considerable refinement and culture. I owe an enormous debt to Eileen Kato, who gave many valuable suggestions at every stage of the translation. She has a special affection for this work, and her late husband, Ambassador Yoshiya Kato, was also a devotee. When he became seriously ill and entered the hospital, he asked his wife to bring him the *Ogura Hyakunin Isshu*, and it was the last book he read before he died. I would like to think that Ambassador Kato and Sachiko Tanabe would be pleased that this great work is appearing in a new English version and hope that it will gain a wider audience. I see this translation as a tribute to them and to the many cultured Japanese whose lives are deeply imbued with delicacy, refinement, and a deep knowledge and understanding of the arts. They are the true heirs of the legacy of the sensibility expressed in the *Ogura Hyakunin Isshu,* and they often pass without due notice.

Near the completion of this translation I accompanied Eileen Kato on a pilgrimage to Kyoto to visit places connected with the work. We visited the ruins of the legendary Shiguretei in Nison-in, where Teika is said to have completed the work in the little hut at the foot of Mount Ogura, which gave the work the name by which it is commonly known by in Japan, the *Ogura Hyakunin Isshu.* We also visited the grave of Teika in Shōkokuji. He lies alongside two other great geniuses, the Muromachi patron of the arts Ashikaga Yoshimasa and the artist Itō Jakuchū. We placed a small bunch of white chrysanthemums on the grave in honor of Teika's love of white. At the time I remember thinking of the extraordinary power of literature. More than six centuries after the death of Teika, two people from more than six thousand miles away were paying homage to the genius of this outstanding poet and editor. Great literature knows no barriers in time or distance. I hope the readers of this translation will gain a small sense of the power and beauty of these poems and even be moved to return to the originals.

INTRODUCTION

The *Ogura Hyakunin Isshu* is a private compilation of poems by the renowned poet and scholar Fujiwara no Teika (1162–1241). Both in English and Japanese, it is often referred to as the *Hyakunin Isshu,* and it is referred to here as such. Said to have been completed around 1237, it was later revised by Teika and his descendents. The editor, Lord Teika, was a supernumerary middle counselor, born into the illustrious noble family of Fujiwara. His father, Shunzei (poem 83), was also a poet and critic, who, in that capacity, held the highest position in the Imperial Court Poetry Bureau and was unrivaled as a poet and critic. in his generation. Lord Teika exceeded even his father, gaining fame not only as a great poet but also as one of the foremost critics and theoreticians of *waka* poetry. He is the representative poet of the Shinkokin period of Japanese literary history, an age named for the eighth imperial anthology that Teika helped compile, the *Shin Kokin Wakashū* (*Shinkokinshū*) (1206). He also compiled and wrote the preface for the *Shin Chokusenshū* (1236).

Fujiwara no Teika was synonymous with Japanese high culture and *waka*, its most acclaimed literary genre, for centuries after his death, and there were many literary and artistic re-inventions of

Figure 1. Portrait of Fujiwara no Teika. Attributed to Fujiwara no Nobuzane. (Shiguretei, Reizei Family Archive)

his poetry and poetics in later periods, most notably at the end of the sixteenth and early seventeenth century. For example, Hosokawa Yūsai (ancestor of the prime minister from 1993 to 1994, Hosokawa Morihiro) and his disciple Karasumaru Mitsuhiro revered him and based their own poetry on his poetic treatises. Great calligraphers, such as Hon'ami Kōetsu, created stunning visual re-inventions of Teika's poems on birds and flowers. Fragments of his idiosyncratic calligraphy were sought after by tea aficionados, who hung them in their tearooms to invoke the spirit of elegance and refinement he represented.

Lord Teika is also important for his work in philology, including the conservation of many important Heian writings such as the *Tale of Genji* and the *Tales of Ise*. His *Maigetsushō* is his *Ars Poetica*, in which he established the canons of poetic taste that remained influential for hundreds of years in Japan. Although said to have been conspicuously ugly and irascible, Teika was recognized as a great poet and authority on and judge of poetry. The *Hyakunin Isshu* is but one of many anthologies Teika compiled during his lifetime, including two imperial anthologies. Most of these were intended as exemplary collections to be used as textbooks on poetry (though this is not the case with this volume) by aristocratic pupils, and they continued to exert great influence for hundreds of years following his demise.

The *Hyakunin Isshu* is a concise history of Japanese poetry from the seventh century to the middle of the twelfth. For hundreds of years, it has been the most widely known and popular collection of Japanese poetry. Along with the *Tales of Ise* and the *Tale of Genji*, the *Hyakunin Isshu* is one of the three most influential classical works of Japanese literature. It has had an inestimable influence on Japanese literature, culture, and visual arts at every level. In the visual arts, for example, every major Japanese print (*ukiyo-e*) artist has illustrated the entire collection. In more recent times, artists such as Shinoda Tōkō have illustrated it. For several hundred years, it has been *the* primer of Japanese classical poetry.

It was also adapted into a popular card game that is still played at the New Year, and these cards have inspired yet another generation of illustrators. The game was already flourishing by the early eighteenth century, and the famous painter Ogata Kōrin's version was created before 1716. The card game was created by dividing these short poems in half and placing the beginning half (*kami no ku*) and the ending half (*shimo no ku*) on small cards. When the first part of the poem was read out, players had to find the endings of the poems, which were spread out on tatami mats. The person who knew the poems by heart could garner the most cards, but some people could win by learning the first syllables of the beginnings and the endings of the poems. Most Japanese in their forties or older learned all these poems by heart and can still recite them. However, for the younger generations the *Hyakunin Isshu* is only read and studied in Japanese literature classes in high schools throughout Japan as a way of acquiring the essentials of classical Japanese grammar necessary for the Japanese university entrance exams. Cultivated Japanese still teach it to their children or grandchildren, and the four-year-old granddaughter of the present Emperor, Princess Aiko, is memorizing the poems.

In classical Japanese poetry, "shi" (詩) generally denoted *kanshi*, poems written in Chinese, whereas in present-day Japanese, "shi" (詩) is a generic term for poetry in general, including both the traditional forms of *waka* and newer forms of poetry employing Western forms. Classical Japanese poetry was generally referred to as *waka*, a term also used for the form now known as *tanka*. But Japanese poetry also includes several other forms, including *chōka*, *katauta*, *sedōka*, *renga*, and haiku. Modern short poems, though written in the same form as traditional *waka*, are almost always referred to as *tanka*. Poems written for the New Year Poetry Reading Ceremony (*utakai hajime*), the annual poetry contest held under the auspices of the

Imperial Household Agency, which selects the topic, are still referred to as *waka*. The *waka* in this volume all share the same form and are composed of five lines, with five syllables in the first and third lines and seven in the others. Topics of the poems were fixed, including the seasons, love, parting, travel, grief and miscellaneous topics. In the translations in this book, *waka* are referred to only by their traditional name *waka* or interchangeably as "poems."

It is easy to read the *Hyakunin Isshu* as a miniature history of Japanese poetry. However, the poems themselves are not easy to understand, not only because many of them have variants but also because of polysemy, which was a central part of the rhetoric and expression of this poetic world. Even by the time Teika was editing them, some of the poems were as much as five hundred years old, so he would have encountered variants and historical shifts in nuance and meaning. Such complications have meant that the Japanese invariably have read the *Hyakunin Isshu* with the aid of countless commentaries written since the thirteenth century. Variations in the commentaries have further complicated interpretations.

Unlike Japanese editions, English translations until Joshua Mostow's monumental *Pictures of the Heart* tended to include as few notes as possible, based on the theory that the essence of a poem can be grasped simply by reading it and that its historical context is extraneous. Mostow, however, convincingly argues that the understanding of a literary work is only enhanced by knowledge of its background and its historical reception. For example, he has studied in detail the differences in interpretation between the poems as they originally appeared and Teika's variations. In cases where there was a divergence between the poem as it originally appeared and Teika's version, I rely on Mostow, and my notes are much indebted to his work. His book greatly facilitated my translation. Rather than attempting to supplement his study, I refer the reader to his work of meticulous scholarship, which will surely be the standard reference work on this text for a generation.

The purpose of my translation is to provide a readable and poetic translation that I hope will open it to a wider readership who will find in these versions something of the depth and beauty of this magical collection. My translation is neither scholarly nor free. I have not tried to confine the translation of the poems to thirty-one syllables as in the original. I have tried in general to follow as closely as possible what is known of Teika's intentions while at the same time making the poems as accessible as possible in English. On a few occasions, I have ignored what is considered his reading and reverted to the original interpretation of the poem. My only claim here is to offer another attempt in the long history of translations of this great work. Others will surely follow in the future.

If I were to compare poetry and translation to the visual arts, then poetry composition would correspond to abstract or figurative painting and translation would correspond to print making. In poetry, one either writes freely in bold dashes (or at least gives one that impression) as in abstract painting or, using venerable techniques, creates figurative images that seem entirely fresh. In translation, one may begin with a bold stroke to capture the heart of the poem, but then one has to return to the original for new applications of color as in the printing of a print. For the latter work, one must be methodical and exact to prevent the loss of a color or its application to an unintended part of the surface. I cannot say that this translation is as exact as a color print, in which each version has been rigorously reapplied to the matrix until a complete image appears. Instead, I would say that it is halfway between a painting and a print, not completely literal in every respect but faithful to the *heart* of the original. It may sometimes be adapted slightly to allow its poetic heart to be expressed in both another language and another age. It is not quite as new as the re-rendering of ancient poems as Teika advocates for poetry writing itself, but informed by his spirit that each new age has its own linguistic and emotional requirements and that these can energize rather than negate the process of translation.

The first translation of the *Hyakunin Isshu*, by Frederick Victor Dickins, was published in 1866; there are more than a dozen translations of this work in English alone. Some scholars argue that we must read the work as Teika intended. I prefer to suggest that a truly great work of art surrenders its ownership and becomes part of the common domain. Indeed, part of the greatness of a work of art or literature lies in its ability to transcend its ownership and allow for new interpretations over time. Multiplicity of interpretation enhances, rather than diminishes, the work.

Teika originally made a slightly different selection of these poems for decorative screens (*byōbu-uta*) of the residence of the father of his daughter-in-law, Utsunomiya Yoritsuna (Renshō), who was the head of one of the chief poetic houses of the Kamakura period. Teika excised the headnotes (*kotobagaki*) that had appeared with these poems in the original anthologies from where he made his selections. These headnotes describe the circumstances in which the poems were composed. Some headnotes merely indicated the topic (*dai*), but others provided long, detailed accounts of the background of the poem's composition, sometimes fictional. However, I have included them in my own notes on the poems, as they add much interesting background narrative The headnotes are not always verifiably correct, but they provide interesting narratives and are part of the historical reception of the poems in the *Hyakunin Isshu* both before and after Teika's version. In the present edition, those headnotes appear at the end of the book so that the reader can encounter the poems without interruption. By including them I hope to make the reader's encounter with the text more informed and pleasurable.

I have also included the Japanese originals and transliterations so that students and the general reader can have access to the originals. The Japanese and transliterated versions are based on

Tadao Shimazu's edition of the *Hyakunin Isshu* (Tokyo: Kadokawa Shoten, 1969) but with some minor differences in orthography. In addition, each poem is accompanied by a calligraphic image of the poem that, apart from its aesthetic appeal, can be used by advanced students to study calligraphy. There are minor textual differences between the printed text and the calligraphic manuscript version. The calligraphic versions that appear on each page as illustrations of the *Hyakunin Isshu* uses the poems for the *Hyakunin Shūka* (the volume that was the predecessor to the *Hyakunin Isshu*), but with the poems of the *Hyakunin Isshu*. This calligraphic text is identical to that of the *Hyakunin Isshu*, but has been rearranged to match the order of the *Hyakunin Isshu* for the purposes of this text.

One difficulty in translating the *Hyakunin Isshu* is that Japanese classical poetry is bound by convention. A list and brief explanation of common literary conventions is in the glossary. One example of the use of convention is that the names of places are codes with fixed associations or signify actions that readers of classical Japanese would have understood. For example, "Osaka" refers to the barrier, not the modern-day city of the same name. It both indicated a place and meant "to meet," especially as in the meeting of lovers. "Naniwa bay" was a place that was famous for meeting pleasure girls. "Reeds cut at Naniwa" signified brevity or brief encounters (including one-night stands). "Kasuga Shrine" was a place where pilgrims went to pray for a safe return before going overseas. For the educated Japanese reader, the mere mention of these place names would immediately evoke such associations.

Some of these language conventions are used in fresh and vivid ways, but they often no longer work well in contemporary English. For example, several poems employ the homonym *miotsukushi*, which can mean both "to wear oneself out" and "a channel marker." The poems play on the idea that one wears oneself out like the wooden channel markers in the sea. However, it is not so easy for the contemporary reader to imagine wearing oneself out like a wooden buoy in this age of plastic, so the play on words cannot have the same metaphorical impact as it would, say, for Teika's first generations of readers, who would immediately recognize the homonym. Most of these conventions are no longer resonant in modern Japanese, either. Sometimes poets themselves found the restrictions of writing *waka* too limiting and opted instead to write poems in Chinese (*kanshi*).

Another difficulty is that some of the poets capture an extremely simple scene with such subtlety that, when translated, the poem seems like a mere image or fragment of a poem rather than a whole poem. The simpler poems on the seasons are especially difficult to translate while preserving the poetic delicacy of the original. However, one of the great strengths of classical Japanese literature is the countless number of *waka* that can express deep emotion and refinement of sensibility in images of profound simplicity. Although some of these images may have lost a part of their resonance simply because the world has changed greatly since the time in which the poems were written, it can be said of all the poems that they are deeply rooted in nature and that many of them contain images so rich and original that they are still fresh a thousand years later.

The choice of using the active or passive voice is another difficulty in rendering classical Japanese into English. Some of the originals contain a deliberate ambiguity as to the subject, that is, the subject marker "I" is excluded. However, modern English poetry, especially post-Romantic poetry, seems unimaginable without a strong subjective voice. Thus I have always placed such versions as the main translation and provided an alternative that might be closer to the original but is weaker as poetry in English, based on my own conviction of what makes for good poetry in English; the reader, of course, is free to disagree.

Not clearly identifying the subject in an English-language poem causes confusion and weakening of the rhetorical structures. I provide the alternate version in the notes to allow the reader to understand the importance of such ambiguity for the original poets. This ambiguity in linguistic expression is one of the beauties and strengths of classical and even contemporary Japanese; in English, while ambiguity also has its own role, a clear subject-marker is essential. For an example of this, see poem 5. In the original, the subject is unclear: It could be either a deer or the poet who is moving into the forest.

Although I hope this translation can be read and enjoyed without any background knowledge, a few points are worth mentioning on the political and cultural background and Teika's principles for selecting, interpreting, and arranging poems: first, Teika's aesthetics, including his predilection for love poetry (dictated in part but not exclusively by convention), his advocacy of the aesthetic concept of *yōen* (a romantic ethereal sentiment), and his love of the color white; second, a brief mention of theories of "association and progression" in the establishment of poetic unity of the text; and, third, the importance for *waka* of the imperial family, court status, and heredity.

Teika relied greatly on his father, Shunzei, to advance his position at court, but he established his literary reputation on his own. Shunzei advocated a literary style of *yūgen* (mystery and depth) and established it as one of the great styles of the age, but Teika and his younger contemporaries preferred the style of *yōen* (ethereal beauty). The most typical example of this style is poem 67 by the Court Handmaid Suō:

> I would be sorry
> to lose my good name
> just because
> I lay my head
> upon your arm

offered as a pillow
for a moment fleeting
as a spring night's dream.

"Spring night," "pillowing arm," and "dream" all combine to create a romantic ethereal sentiment typical of the *yōen* aesthetic. *Yōen* celebrates fleeting and dreamlike encounters portrayed in a mysterious atmosphere. Other characteristics of *yōen* are subtle allusions to classical Chinese and Japanese tales that create narrative or "talelike" qualities, elements of the surreal, especially surreal landscapes. The concept of *yōen* certainly influenced Teika's selection and interpretation of poems in this collection, but to what extent has not been established definitively. It should be pointed out that the aesthetic of *yōen* occupied Teika only during his youth and until middle age. During his forties, he seems to have suffered a poetic drought, which he writes about in the preface to *Kindai Shūka* (Superior Poems of Our Times). He recovered his poetic stature in his fifties but thereafter is said to have abandoned *yōen* in favor of a new stylistic ideal, *ushin* (conviction of feeling), a starker style favoring greater immediacy and intensity of passion over remote beauty.[1]

Much has been written about the color white in Teika's poetry, clearly his favorite color. Just as we speak of Rikyū gray in the Japanese tea ceremony or Issey Miyake black in contemporary Japanese fashion, it is worth recognizing Teika's contribution to the establishment of white as a color of refinement, purity, elegance, and sophistication in the aesthetic sensibility of the Japanese. I believe that the color white is also a key element of the beauty of *yōen*. There is a predominance of pure white and pale scenes, of cloud or mist or fog or moonlight. At least ten poems employ images of white, and on many occasions white on white. In poem 29, one of Teika's favorites, included in several collections,

Ōshikōchi no Mitsune writes of his inability to distinguish white chrysanthemums from the first frost:

> I can only pluck at random
> for I cannot tell apart
> in all this whiteness—
> white chrysanthemums
> from the first frost.

An exquisite image evokes a natural world of great beauty and purity.

Another poem describes a poet sailing out on white-crested waves, only to turn around and suddenly see something much whiter—snow falling on the peak of Mt. Fuji. Poem 76 describes the poet's inability to distinguish between white waves and far-off clouds. Poem 6 invokes a magical scene of white frost settling on the Bridge of Magpie Wings. As magpie wings have white stripes on them, one can see here another of the almost surreal white-on-white *yōen*-like atmospheric settings evoked. Poem 37 compares white dewdrops to unstrung pearls. In addition, several poems depict the pale white moon of dawn, cherry blossoms, the white robes of Summer, fog, mist, and snow. Poem 96 humorously compares white blossoms to snow, only to reveal that, in fact, the whiteness is the white hair of old age.

It is worth mentioning as well the theory of association and progression first advocated in an article by Konishi Jin'ichi and later adapted by Brower and Miner, especially in their translation of Teika's *Kindai Shūka* (Superior Poems of Our Time). According to this theory, Japanese court poetry collections are all integrally unified by principles of association and progression. Progression refers to the temporal and chronological sequence of events following the changing seasons, the court calendar of events, and the movement of a love affair from brief fulfillment to betrayal

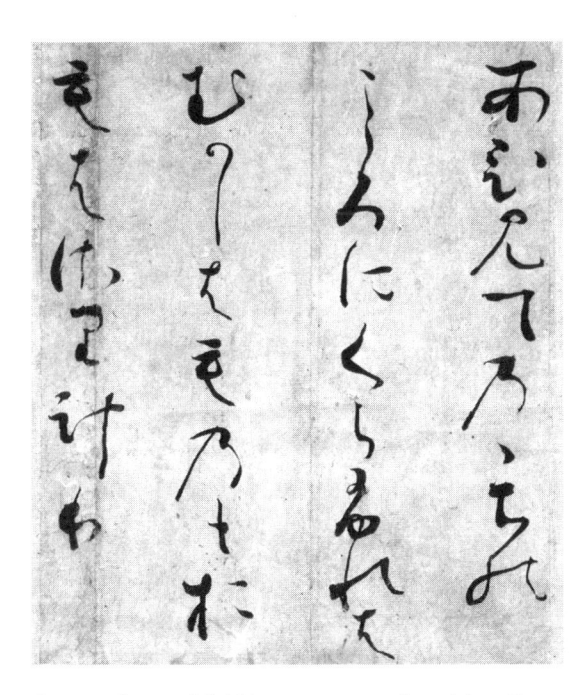

Figure 2. Ogura shikishi, *poem 43 from the anthology* Ogura Hyakunin Isshu. *Calligraphy attributed to Fujiwara no Sadaie (1162–1241). Ink on paper, Kamakura period (thirteenth century). (Gotoh Museum)*

and despair. Association refers to integration achieved by means of interrelated imagery, for example, poems invoking the same place name, such as Yoshino or Naniwa, a repetition of poems on the same theme, such as the coldness of dawn partings, or ones employing the same or similar imagery. Several poems speak of the Tatsuta river and its famed autumn colors (poems 17 and 69) both at the beginning and near the end of that work by association with yet other poems on autumn colors (see poems 24 and 26). Allusions and repeated use of rhetorical techniques can also achieve this effect. In the *Hyakunin Isshu*, for example, *shirotae*, a pillow word for white, is repeated in two poems (2 and 4). In this case, the poems are deliberately placed closer to each other for greater resonance.

According to Brower and Miner, the arrangement of the poems in *Superior Poems of Our Times* is marked by the poet's predilection for love poetry, especially on the darker aspects of love, such as betrayal, abandonment, bitterness, and despair. Their translation is arranged to show a progressive development and interaction between the poems, which encourages a reading of the work as an integrated and unified whole. Of the one hundred poems in the *Hyakunin Isshu*, more than forty are love poems, in part surely because of convention but in part also because of Teika's belief in the importance of love. At the same time, it should be pointed out that in later work on Teika, Brower (this time writing alone) at least partially disavows the theory that there is a progressive development and interaction between the poems and argues for a looser reading of the texts. In addition, he suggests that the poems be read more as individual items than for their thematic interconnectedness.

Given that Teika was one of the editorial geniuses of his age, it is common sense that in a work such as the *Hyakunin Isshu* one would expect strong principles of unity, both implicit and explicit. Yet research on the exact nature and extent of the principles of unity remains inconclusive. Definitive answers to many questions are not available and may never be. If anything can be asserted with certainty, it is that if there is an answer it is surely in the poems themselves: Repeated reading might reveal Teika's central preoccupations as editor. My own instinct tells me that Teika's thinking remains elusive and will never be fully accessible to us. While editing he was moved by both highly conscious yet also deeply unconscious forces, but his central message is like that of W. B. Yeats's reprimand to his compatriot poets: "Irish Poets! Learn your trade." To do that, one must return repeatedly to the model poems themselves.

This collection shows how Teika defines himself in relation to the poetic tradition that he both inherits and promulgates. We can chart a map of his poetic imagination, trace aspects of the development of his poetic sensibility, and partially understand his editorial genius. According to Emperor GoToba, Teika was dictatorial in all matters relating to poetry and editing, but eight hundred years of history have consistently proved his judgments right.

Regarding the importance of the imperial family to *waka*, one can easily see the *Hyakunin Isshu* as an encomium to imperial reign. Furthermore, for Teika, the imperials are themselves both accomplished practitioners and the spiritual patrons of *waka*. Heredity is of importance not only for the ruling emperors but also for the poets. Thirty-four of the one hundred poets represented in the collection are related to one another by direct lines of descent, so heredity obviously played an extremely important part in the selection process. The importance of heredity perhaps explains why even some minor poets, particularly imperial ones, are included. Heredity, status at court, and poetic ability were all inseparable in the world of the Heian and Kamakura nobility. The Kamakura nobility caused trouble for the imperial family, and it is interesting to note that only one of them is included in the *Hyakunin Isshu*. But the inclusion of the third Kamakura shogun, Minamoto no Sanetomo in the *Hyakunin Isshu* (poem 93) is surely based on his poetic and not his political supremacy. Teika had been his tutor and declared his pupil's poetry superior to his own. Although one might suspect that there would be no love lost between Sanetomo and GoToba, they were actually close and enjoyed a literary correspondence. Sanetomo's assassination was said to have served in part to spur GoToba to rebellion.

The *Hyakunin Isshu* includes poems by eight emperors. The number eight is considered auspicious in both Chinese and Japanese culture. Unlike its representation in the arabic number system (8), which is a closed symbol, the written representation in Chinese and Japanese is 八. This character is an open symbol, with neither beginning nor end; in the Sino-Japanese tradition, it is also a symbol for longevity, in this case signifying the long reign of the imperial family. The *Hyakunin Isshu* covers almost six centuries of Japanese history, from the reign of Emperor Tenji (626–671; r. 629–641) to Emperor Juntoku (1197–1242; r. 1211–1221). The eight emperors whose poetry appears in the volume were not chosen at random. The *Hyakunin Isshu* opens with two emperors and again closes with two emperors, both parent-child pairs, but this is relevant primarily because of the importance of these individuals for poetry. In addition, several combinations of parent-child poets also emphasize heredity and continuity.

In 1996 considerable interest was aroused when the Reizei family in Kyoto published an earlier version of their ancestor Teika's *Hyakunin Isshu*, with some selections different from those made for the version he is thought to have presented to Rensho *(Hyakunin Shuuka)*. For example, in the *Hyakunin Shuuka*, the final two poems were not by the two emperors. It was long thought that the version Teika gave to Rensho represented his final selection, and theories abounded as to how the *Hyakunin Isshu* eventually came into its current form. One such theory proposes that the poems of the two emperors were added at Teika's request posthumously by his descendants. This new discovery from the Reizei family archives, however, suggests that Teika made the selections and completed the collection himself. Teika was not on good terms with GoToba, but the latter, particularly while in exile, developed into a first-rate poet— and for Teika poetry mattered most. Perhaps Teika overlooked their personal differences when he encountered GoToba's development as a poet. But it is also likely that Teika wanted to have eight emperors represented because eight is a symbol of eternity, and thus including the work of eight emperors in the volume expresses an implicit wish for the imperial line to continue forever.

The thirty-eighth Emperor Tenji, whose *waka* opens the volume, not only was the first emperor for whom a reliable historic record remains but also was the sovereign who ennobled the Fujiwara family and gave them their illustrious clan name. Thus the first poems simultaneously celebrate the imperial line, the beginning of *waka*, and the beginning of the Fujiwara family. In his general layout of the *Hyakunin Isshu*, Teika can be seen to acknowledge a deep family debt to Tenji and his descendants. But, of greater importance for the *Hyakunin Isshu*, Emperor Tenji, a great patron of poets and poetry, was himself an accomplished Man'yō poet. He was the first to establish the close links between the imperial court and the world of poetry that are faithfully fostered to this day.

The second poet to appear in the *Hyakunin Isshu* is Emperor Jitō, a female emperor. She was not highly regarded as an emperor, but carried on her father's patronage of poets and poetry and helped Hitomaro in particular. No doubt her inclusion in the *Hyakunin Isshu* owes to her importance as a patron of poetry.

The third poem in the *Hyakunin Isshu* is by Hitomaro, famous for his unconditional loyalty to Emperor Jitō and the imperial family, who is revered as a deity of poetry. Hitomaro regarded Jitō as a goddess in a way no later poets regarded members of the imperial family and so his inclusion following two emperors may be seen as a tribute to him by Teika. The *Hyakunin Isshu* closes with Emperor Juntoku (1197–1242), preceded by his father, Emperor GoToba (1180–1239). GoToba is preceded by Fujiwara no Ietaka, a fine poet and known for his unswerving loyalty to his sovereign even after his banishment to the island of Oki. The great link between him and his sovereign was poetry.

Yet Teika also realized that the world of *waka* had become the too exclusive apanage of the court elite and wanted to open up its ranks to people of lower status. Both GoToba and his son, Juntoku, were deeply interested in the new *renga*, which drew on the talents of nonaristocratic poets. But both were banished men. They had rebelled against the new Kamakura shogunate in the Jōkyū Rebellion of 1221. It was politically incorrect and a great risk to show them honor during the time of the administration that banished them. But Teika could be expected to want to include them in the *Hyakunin Isshu*. It is certainly conceivable that for this reason Teika had to delay his final selections because of political exigencies and had asked that his real choices be added later.

The other four emperors were also chosen for their significance in the world of poetry. For example, Emperor Yōzei (868–949), the fifty-seventh sovereign, ascended the throne in childhood, but he was deposed after reigning for only eight years because he was said to have shown signs of mental instability. However, for the next sixty years, he was an assiduous practitioner of poetry and arranged poetic contests and helped poets and poetry in many ways. Only one of his poems is extant—the one in the *Hyakunin Isshu*.

In addition to the eight emperors, the collection includes works by four children of emperors, one of them the Princess Shokushi, four grandsons of emperors, and two great-grandsons. Represented are twenty-five Fujiwaras so named and others, priests or women who were of Fujiwara descent. Here too it is clear that Teika was not simply engaging in nepotism but, rather, making selections for poetry's sake. No one can deny that the Fujiwara clan produced many outstanding poets. Teika was also clearly paying tribute to the selection of poets by his predecessors. Notable is his inclusion in the *Hyakunin Isshu* of twenty-four out of the thirty-six reputed poets chosen by his ancestor, Fujiwara no Kintō.

This, then, was a thoroughly blueblood, elitist, and exclusive group that talented outsiders tried to emulate by creating sequences of linked poetry (*renga*), which was based on *waka* but had even more strict rules. It was, however, open to everyone and to be played as a social entertainment by two or more people. Even as late as the fifteenth century, the great *renga* master Priest Sōgi was deeply frustrated at not being accepted in the world of *waka*.[2] He was one of the key figures who raised *renga* to new levels of excellence and dignity, preparing the way for haiku, which developed from the opening stanza (*hokku*) of *renga*. Bashō (1644–1694) recognized the *waka* and *renga* giants Saigyō (1118–1190) and Sōgi (1424–1502) as his masters.

Emperor Meiji opened the gates of the *waka* world, and since then the New Year Poetry Reading Ceremony (*utakai hajime*) has welcomed *waka* from commoners all over Japan and overseas and even from non-Japanese. Yet, despite the opening of the world of *waka* to commoners, the tie is still very strongly maintained with the palace. All members of the imperial family continue to write *waka* throughout the year, and their *waka* are read at the annual New Year Poetry Reading Ceremony, along with ten *waka* selected from contributions of the general public. The reading is held at the palace as part of the New Year celebrations.

Other aspects of the Japanese tradition celebrated in the *Hyakunin Isshu* are also still celebrated. For example, the first poem in the collection depicts the emperor as a rice farmer. There are conflicting theories as to when exactly the tradition of the emperor as rice farmer was established. Some historians argue that the tradition was a Meiji invention, and others that it was a Meiji re-invention, but this tradition was clearly referred to much earlier (such as in the first poem in the *Hyakunin Isshu*), and certainly since the Meiji period the emperor has been officially recognized as a symbolic rice farmer and father of the nation. As in the first poem of the *Hyakunin Isshu*, the emperor's duties include sharing the work and worry of his subjects. I have seen the ricefield on the palace grounds, where His Majesty, Emperor Akihito, plants and tends rice that is used in the rice harvest ceremonies every year. He sows the seed, transplants the seedlings, carefully tends the growing crop, and reaps and harvests the ripe grain. The rice is then used in the Niinamesai, Feast of the First Fruits.

Finally, it is worth mentioning a few points on women, ekphrasis (i.e., poems about paintings or combinations of poems and illustrations) and topography in the *Hyakunin Isshu*. Women feature prominently in this collection. In addition to Jitō, it features twenty women, including all the great family names of Heian times, many of them ladies-in-waiting to famous consorts of emperors. However, their prominence in this collection owes not to their sex but to the abundance of outstanding female poets during the Heian period. Almost all the most layered, emotionally dense, and linguistically complex poems in this collection are by women, in particular poems 9, 60, and 62. An appendix to poem 9 demonstrates the complexity of the poet's achievement (see Appendix). Some of the women in the collection are represented by sentimental poems, but others are represented by masterpieces virtually impossible to translate because they are so rich in clever multilayered wordplay and, at the same time, so full of deep and intense emotion.

Teika also chose many poems that celebrate aspects of place names that are puns and places in the locality of the actual place where Teika is said to have edited the volume, such as poem 55, which celebrates an ancient waterfall at nearby Daikakuji that has long since ceased to flow. Perhaps he was thinking of adding illustrations of the poems later and therefore chose those that had intensely visual images, or his selection may have been a function of Teika's own intensely visual sensibility.[3]

My interest in the *Hyakunin Isshu* was aroused in part by my interest in ekphrasis, that is, poems about paintings or visual images or the combination of visual and literary depiction. Japanese literature is intensely ekphratic, with countless renderings of poems combined with visual depictions on a great variety of media and genre, from the famous poem pictures (*shigajiku*) of the Muromachi period to the outstanding lacquer ware of the Momoyama and Edo periods. In Japan, poem and painting have commonly been paired since the Heian period. In Western culture, ekphrasis mostly means poems about paintings but in Japan there are also countless examples of paintings based on literary works. It is one of the most striking characteristics of Japanese literature.

During the period in which the *Hyakunin Isshu* was edited, the most common pairing was of poems written on squares of decorative paper (*shikishi*) and then affixed to screens (*byōbu*), known as "screen poems" (*byōbu-uta*). There is clear evidence that the poets based at least part of their poems on the images depicted on the screens, rather than on scenes from the real world, and that word and image were treated as an integral whole. At other times, the poet wrote as if he was himself the figure depicted in the scene on the screen, and, upon completing the poem, affixed it to the screen near the image. There is a possibility that the cartouches of the *Hyakunin Isshu* were pictorializations of the poems. Teika, for example, mentions poem-pictures (*uta-e*) in his diary and was asked to compose poems for other screens of famous places (*meisho-e*), for example, poems for screens that were used for the Saisho-In temple commissioned by retired Emperor Gotoba in 1207. He was also commissioned to write poems on birds and flowers of the twelve months for the private residence of the Cloistered Prince Dōjo in 1214 (Mostow, *Pictures of the Heart*, 95).

The evidence clearly suggests that Teika, like other poets of the period, often composed poems based on visual images. Mostow has done the most research on this topic, and his various articles are recommended for further reading. However, he does not use the term "ekphrasis," and I have not seen it elsewhere in writing on the relationship of Japanese art and literature. These days there is a great quantity of ekphratic poetry written by English-speaking poets, but I think that the concept of ekphrasis is a highly useful one for understanding the complex relationship of art in literature of Japan, particularly if we expand the concept to contain its opposite, that is, not only poems about paintings but also paintings about poems. There are many reasons for the number of paintings about poems, such as the brevity of the poems and their tendency to employ one single striking image. But another reason is surely the Japanese artists' love of depicting not only real scenes but also scenes of the heart.

Most of the poems in this collection are highly visual, and in a few cases I have arranged the words of the translation to evoke visually the image of the scene described in the poem. For example, I suggest a waterfall by leaving a blank space between lines to convey the idea of water falling. For examples of these word-picture translations, see poems 3, 17, and 32.

There are thousands of editions of the *Hyakunin Isshu* both as text and card game and the traditional way they are presented is with an illustration either of the poet or some scene depicted in the poem accompanying calligraphic versions by hand or in woodblock print. Woodblock print versions were disseminated widely in the Edo period, and it is mostly these editions that still survive. Some of the card games editions are early examples of mixed media. For example, the collection of cards that illustrates this book is a printed text, but the illustrations were then painted in delicate wash colors by hand. It would be lovely to illustrate this edition with elegant drawings from the period in which it was edited, but they do not exist, and I do not think the merchant class taste of Edo that produced thousands of woodblock print editions captures well the sensibility of the court culture of Teika. For this edition, I did manage to find the simple, elegant, but also charming line drawings of the poets that accompany the poems and some elegant calligraphy. Although they are of differing periods, they go well together. The accompaniment of calligraphy and image is the conventional way to present this text, but the calligraphy will also be useful for advanced students of Japanese in studying written Japanese.

The translation of this work was prompted in part by a personal quest to learn more about Japan and the Japanese. All the poems in the collection might not be of the first rank, but the finest reveal the subtle aesthetic sensibility of the Japanese at its most sophisticated and refined. More specifically, I found in the text many aspects that are evident in contemporary Japanese culture, such as subtlety in verbal expression, indirectness, an intensely visual nature, great emotional reserves, a capacity for deep and profound emotion, and the tendency to be both complex and elusive in emotional expression. Haiku is widely known in the West, but haiku originally developed from *waka*. As mentioned above, the term was originally *hokku*, the opening stanza of *renga*. Haiku came into being when the starting verse came to exist independently from the linked verse. Formally, it is the equivalent of the upper strophe of *waka*, namely, having lines of five, seven, five syllables, respectively, for a total of seventeen. Although haiku developed in a completely different way from *waka*, a study of Japanese *waka* is helpful for understanding more about haiku and how to write it. When Shunzei noted, "All who come to our land study this poetry; all who live in our land compose it," he was speaking of *waka*, not haiku.[4] Thus, if one wants to understand the heart of the Japanese, it could equally be argued that it is found not only in haiku, but also—or even more so—in *waka*. I hope that the translation of this venerable collection will provide a good introduction for that purpose. It is my wish, too, that one day the word *waka* will become as common in English as "haiku." Just as translations of haiku have provided an impetus to poets writing in English I hope that the translation of *waka* can provide a similar impetus and even expand the possibilities of writing poetry in English. As I so happily discovered myself, I have a final suggestion: If you want to understand the Japanese, read the *Hyakunin Isshu*.

Peter McMillan
Lake Yamanaka

Notes

1. *For additional information, see Donald Keene's* Seeds in the Heart: Japanese Literature from Earliest Times to the Late Sixteenth Century, *the introduction to Joshua Mostow's* Pictures of the Heart, *and Konishi Jin'ichi's* A History of Japanese Literature, *Vol. 3:* The High Middle Ages, *pp. 214–216, which includes translations of poetry contests and Teika's comments on them. Also recommended are Robert H. Brower and Earl Miner's many texts on Japanese classical literature, including* Fujiwara Teika's Superior Poems of Our Time (Kindai Shūka), *a translation and commentary on one of Teika's treatises on poetry.*

2. *Sōgi, "Tsukushi no Michi no Ki" (Pilgrimage to Dazaifu), trans. Eileen Kato,* Monumenta Nipponica *34:3 (Autumn 1979): 364.*

3. *For further reading on the poem-picture tradition, see Mostow's* Pictures of the Heart, *which gives a detailed account, focusing on the Edo period. Carolyn Wheelright, in* Word in Flower: The Visualization of Classical Literature in Seventeenth-Century Japan, *gives a fascinating account of the revival of Teika in seventeenth-century art and culture.*

4. *Shunzei (also read Toshinari) (1114–1204), the father of Fujiwara no Teika, in his* Korai Fūtaishō *(1197) a treatise on poetry-writing and the history of* waka *(adapted from Kato's translation of Sōgi's "Pilgrimage to Dazaifu").*

THE POEMS

1. EMPEROR TENJI

In the harvest field
gaps in the rough-laid thatch
of my makeshift hut
let the dewdrops in,
but it is not only dew
that wets my sleeves
through this long night alone.

2. EMPEROR JITŌ

Spring has passed.
At last the mists have risen
and white robes of summer
are being aired
on fragrant Mount Kagu—
beloved of the gods.

3. KAKINOMOTO NO HITOMARO

The
long
tail
of
the
copper
pheasant
trails—
drags
on
and
on
like
this
long
night
in
the
lonely
mountains
where
like
that
bird
I
too
must
sleep
without
my
love.

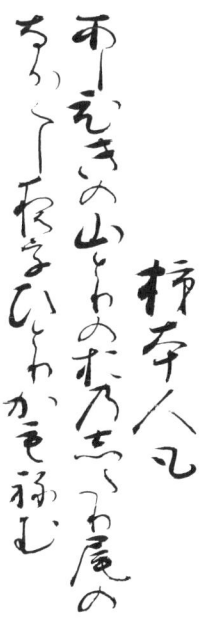

4. YAMABE NO AKAHITO

Sailing out on the white crests
of the Bay of Tago, I look up.
There before me
even more dazzling—
snow still falling
on Fuji crowned in white.

5. SARUMARU DAYŪ

Autumn at its saddest—
Rustling through the leaves
and moving on alone
deep into the mountains,
I hear the lonely stag
belling for his doe.

6. ŌTOMO NO YAKAMOCHI

How the night deepens.
As lovers part
a white ribbon of frost
is stretched along
the Bridge of Magpie Wings.

7. ABE NO NAKAMARO

When I look up
into the vast sky tonight,
is it the same moon
that I saw rising
from behind Mt. Mikasa
at Kasuga Shrine
all those years ago?

8. PRIEST KISEN

My dwelling is a hut
in the southeast of the capital.
People talk of me as the one
who fled the sorrows of the world
only to end up on the Hill of Sorrow
living alone with deer.

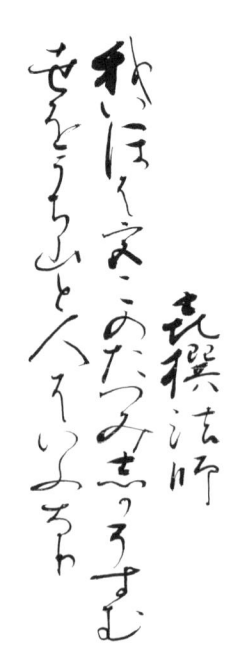

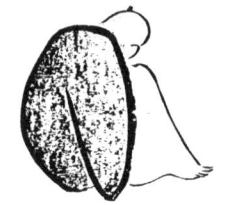

9. ONO NO KOMACHI

A life in vain.
My looks, talents faded
like these cherry blossoms
paling in the endless rains
that I gaze out upon, alone.

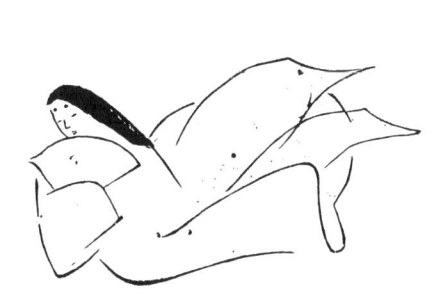

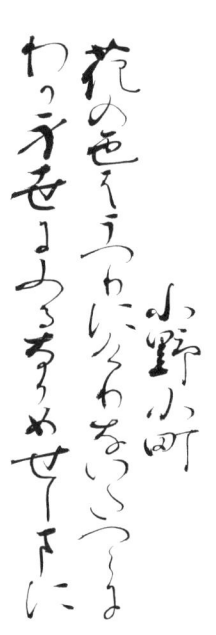

10. SEMIMARU

So this is the place!
The crowds,
coming
going
meeting
parting;
friends
strangers,
known
unknown—
The Osaka Barrier

11. ONO NO TAKAMURA

Fishing boats upon this sea!
Tell whoever asks
I am being rowed away to exile
out past the many islets
to the vast ocean beyond.

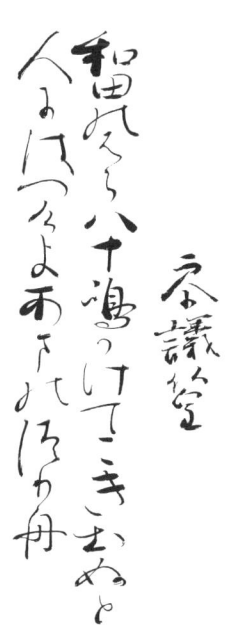

12. ARCHBISHOP HENJŌ

Breezes of Heaven!
Blow closed the pathway
through the clouds,
to keep a little longer
these heavenly
maiden dancers
from returning home.

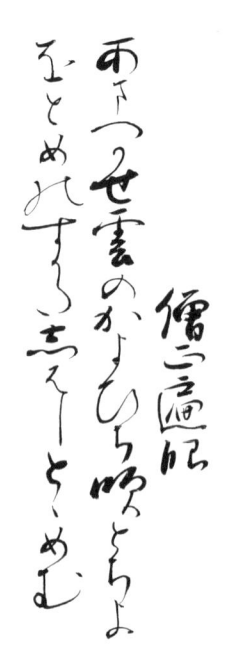

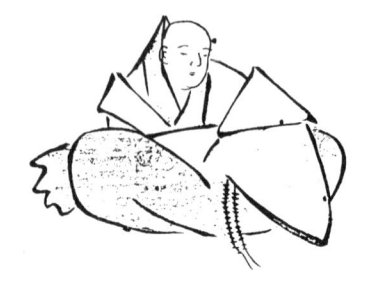

13. RETIRED EMPEROR YŌZEI

Like the Minano River
surging from the peak
of Mt. Tsukuba,
my love cascades
to make deep pools
below the falls.

14. MINAMOTO NO TŌRU

With the pain
of this secret love
my heart is full
of tangled thoughts
like the wild fern patterns
dyed on Shinobu cloth
of the far off north.
Since it is not my fault
whose is it . . . ?

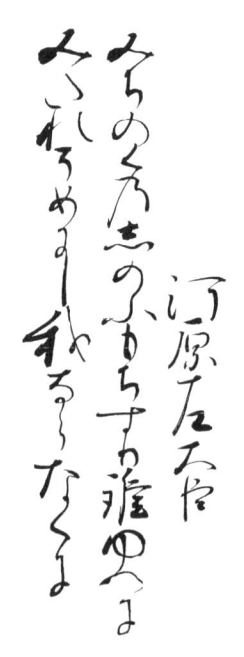

15. EMPEROR KŌKŌ

For you,
I went out to the fields
to pick the first spring greens—
all the while on my sleeves
a light snow falling.

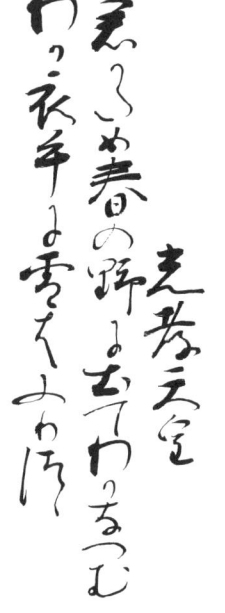

16. ARIWARA NO YUKIHIRA

Though I may leave
for Mt. Inaba,
famous for the pines
covering its peak,
if I hear you pine for me
I'll come straight home to you.

17. ARIWARA NO NARIHIRA

Even the almighty
gods of old
never knew
such beauty:
on the river Tatsuta
in autumn sunlight
a brocade—

reds flowing above,

blue water below.

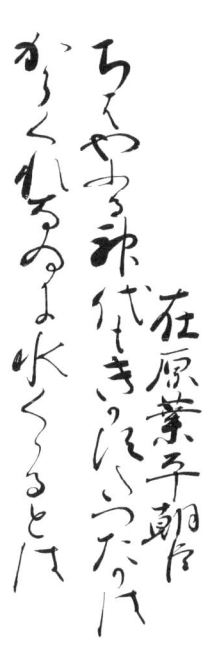

18. FUJIWARA NO TOSHIYUKI

Unlike the waves
beating on the shores
of Sumiyoshi Bay,
you whom I long to meet
avoid the eyes of others
and refuse to come to me,
even at night,
even on the road of dreams.

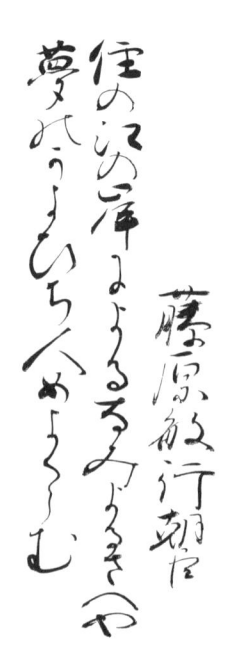

19. ISE

Are you saying that
not even for the short space
between the nodes of a reed
in the Naniwa Inlet
we should go through life
and never meet again?

20. PRINCE MOTOYOSHI

Like Naniwa's
channel markers
whose name means
'self-sacrifice,'
I, too, would
give my life
just to see you
once again.

21. PRIEST SOSEI

Just because you said,
'I'm coming right away,'
I waited for you
all through the late
autumn night,
but only the moon
came to greet me
at the cold light of dawn!

22. FUN'YA NO YASUHIDE

The mountain wind
has just to blow
and the leaves
and grasses of autumn
wither and die.
That must be why
the character for 'storm'
also means 'destroyer'!

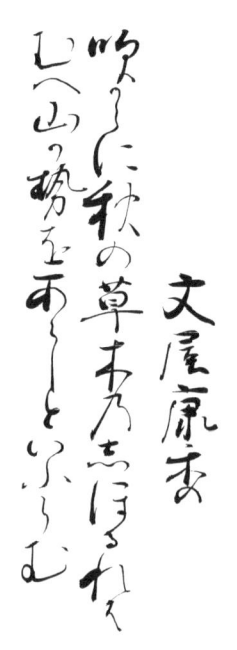

23. ŌE NO CHISATO

Looking at the moon
thoughts of a thousand things
fill me with sadness—
but autumn's dejection
does not come to me alone.

24. SUGAWARA NO MICHIZANE

On this journey
I have no streamers
made of silk to offer up.
Gods, if it pleases you,
may you take instead
this beautiful brocade
of Mt. Tamuke's
autumn colors.

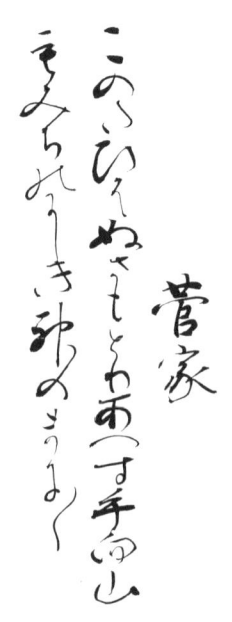

25. FUJIWARA NO SADAKATA

If it is true to its name,
the 'let-us-sleep-together vine,'
that grows on Meeting Hill,
how I wish I could
draw you in to me
—like a tendril of that vine—
unknown to anyone.

26. FUJIWARA NO TADAHIRA

Mt. Ogura,
if you have a heart
please wait
for the emperor
to pass this way
before shedding
on the peak
your lovely
autumn colors.

27. FUJIWARA NO KANESUKE

When was it
I got my first glimpse?
Like the Moor of Jars
divided by the Izumi river,
I am split in two—
so deep my longing for you.

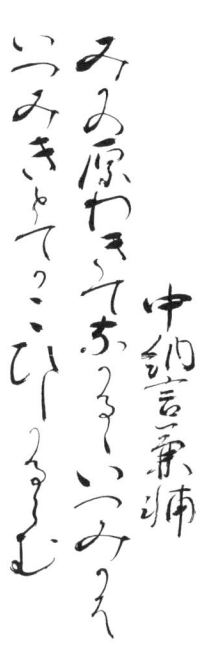

28. MINAMOTO NO MUNEYUKI

In this mountain village
it is in winter
that I feel loneliest—
both grasses
and visitors
dry up.

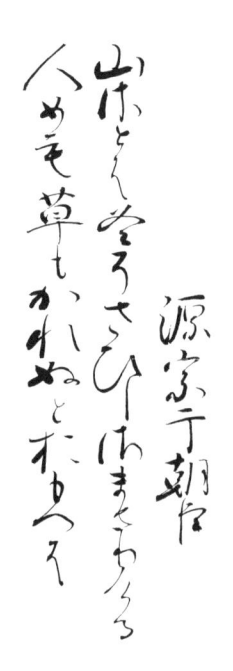

29. ŌSHIKŌCHI NO MITSUNE

I can only pluck at random
for I cannot tell apart
in all this whiteness—
white chrysanthemums
from the first frost.

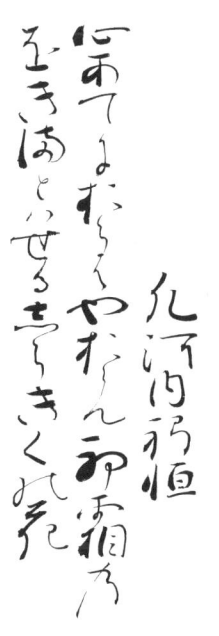

30. MIBU NO TADAMINE

Nothing is so miserable
as the hour before dawn
since I parted from you—
The look on your face then
cold as the morning moon.

31. SAKANOUE NO KORENORI

The first light
over Yoshino village—
The snow has piled
so deep, so white
I cannot tell it from the
dawn's pale moonlight.

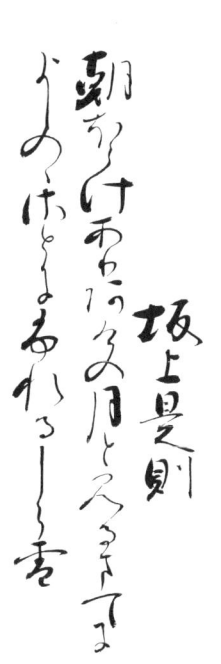

32. HARUMICHI NO TSURAKI

The weir the wind
has flung across
the mountain stream
blocking the flow

is made of autumn's
richly colored leaves.

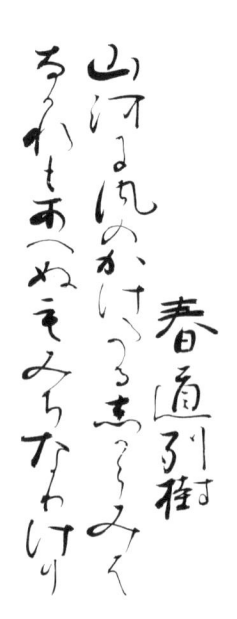

33. KI NO TOMONORI

Cherry blossoms,
on this quiet
lambent day
of spring,
why do you scatter
with such unquiet hearts?

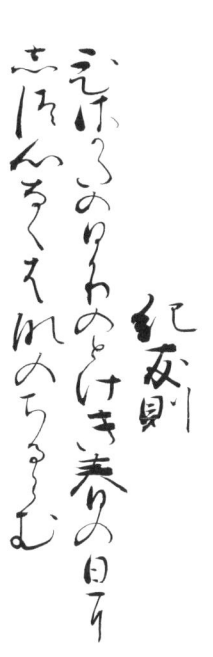

34. FUJIWARA NO OKIKAZE

What dear friends do I have
to confide in now?
Only the aged pine
of Takasago
has my years, I think.
But, alas, he is not
an old friend of mine.

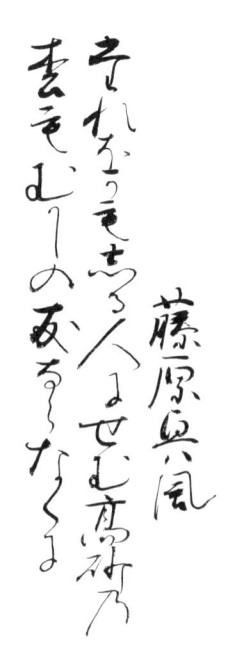

35. KI NO TSURAYUKI

Have you changed?
I cannot read your heart.
But at least I know
that here in my old home
as always the plum blossom
blooms with fragrance
of the past.

36. KIYOHARA NO FUKAYABU

Summer night!
Though it still seems
early evening,
dawn has already come.
Even the moon
could not make it
to her setting.
Where in the clouds
will she rest?

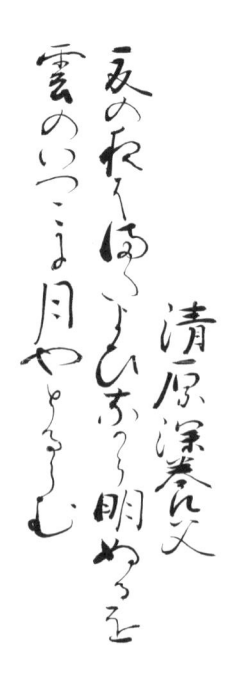

37. FUN'YA NO ASAYASU

When the wind gusts
over the autumn fields
the glistening white dewdrops
lie strewn about
like scattered pearls.

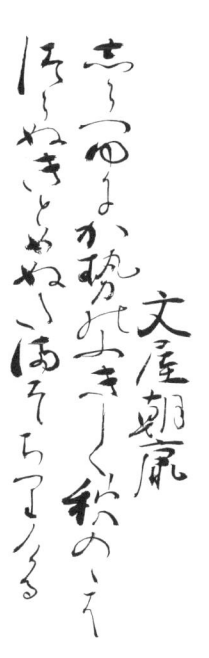

38. UKON

Though you have
forgotten about us,
I do not think of myself.
But how I fear for you,
who swore to the gods
of your undying love for me.

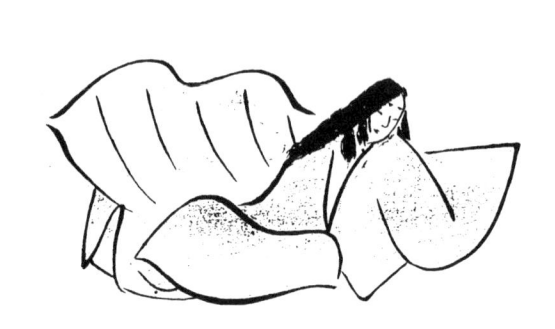

39. MINAMOTO NO HITOSHI

Though I scarcely show
my secret feelings
like those few reeds
sprouting unnoticed
in low bamboo,
they are too much
for me to hide.
Why do I love you so?

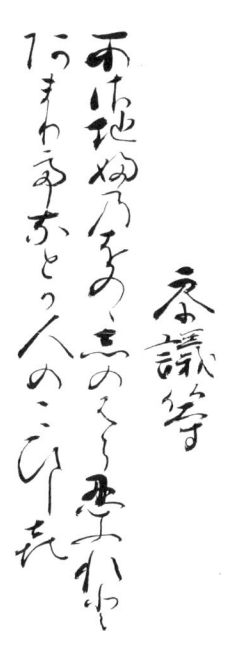

40. TAIRA NO KANEMORI

Though I try to keep it secret,
my deep love
shows in the blush on my face.
Others keep asking me
—*Who* are you thinking of?

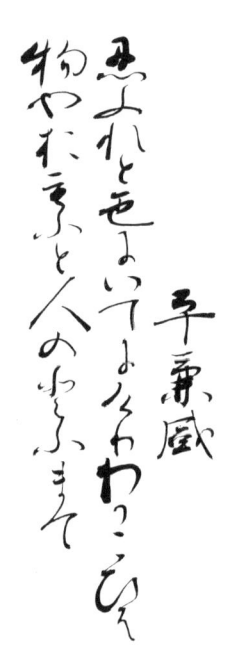

41. MIBU NO TADAMI

My name's been raised;
already rumors are rife.
Though we have just met,
and I thought no one knew about
my newfound love!

42. KIYOHARA NO MOTOSUKE

We pledged our love.
Wringing tears
from our sleeves,
we both vowed
nothing would part us,
not even if great waves
engulfed the pines
of Mount Forever.

43. FUJIWARA NO ATSUTADA

How I longed for you
before we had made love.
Yet when I compare
my heart since then
to what it was before
I know I had not grasped at all
what it is to love.

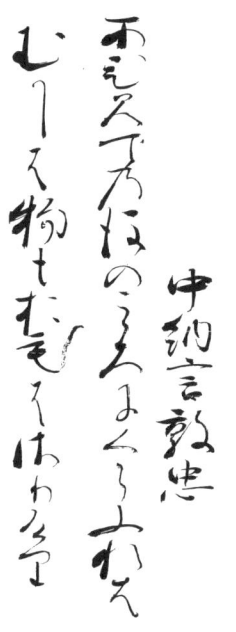

44. FUJIWARA NO ASATADA

It is not that I regret
that we have loved.
But I would not feel
so desolate now
about your cruelty
had we never met at all.

45. FUJIWARA NO KOREMASA

'I feel so sorry for you!'—
No one comes to mind
who would say that to me.
Does it mean
I must die sad, alone?

46. SONE NO YOSHITADA

Crossing the Straits of Yura
the boatman lost the rudder.
The boat's adrift
not knowing where it goes.
Is the course of love like this?

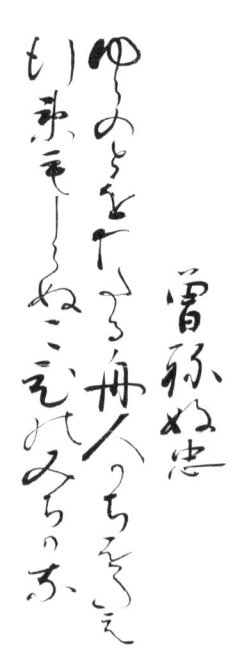

47. PRIEST EGYŌ
(SOMETIMES READ EKEI)

How lonely this house
overgrown with goosegrass weeds.
No one visits me—
only the weary autumn comes.

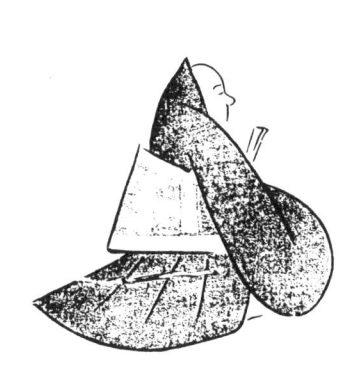

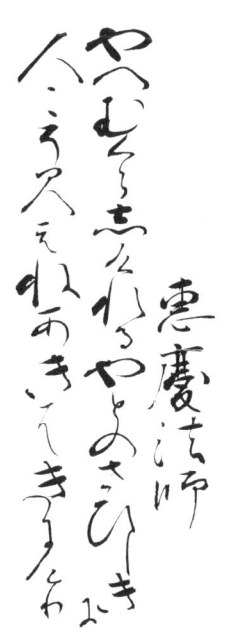

48. MINAMOTO NO SHIGEYUKI

In the fierce wind
the waves beat upon,
but are held by rocks.
Yet my beloved will not brake
these turbulent thoughts of love
pounding upon my heart.

49. ŌNAKATOMI NO YOSHINOBU

The watch fires of the palace guards
blaze by the gates at night
become embers in the day
like my love
which wanes by day
and burns by night.

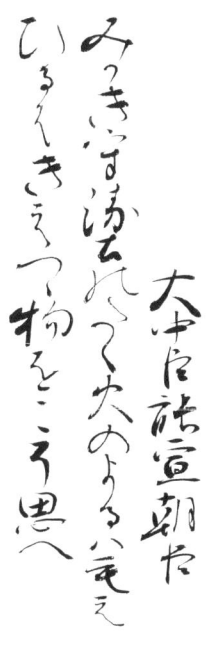

50. FUJIWARA NO YOSHITAKA

I always thought
I would give my life
to meet you only once,
but now, having spent a night
with you, I wish that I may
go on living forever.

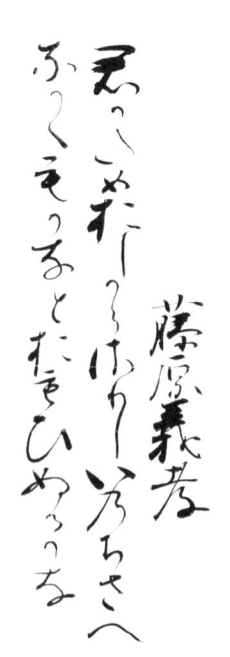

51. FUJIWARA NO SANEKATA

Can I let you know
what consumes me?
Unknown to you,
my heart blazes
like red hot moxa
aflame with love
for you.

52. FUJIWARA NO MICHINOBU

As the sun rises
I know that when
it sets at night
I can see you again.
Yet even so, how hateful—
Parting in this cold light of dawn.

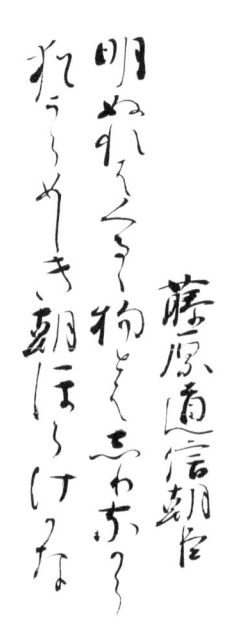

53. MOTHER OF MICHITSUNA

Longing for you
I spend whole nights
lamenting. But one like you
can hardly know
how long a night would be
till it breaks at dawn—
if spent alone.

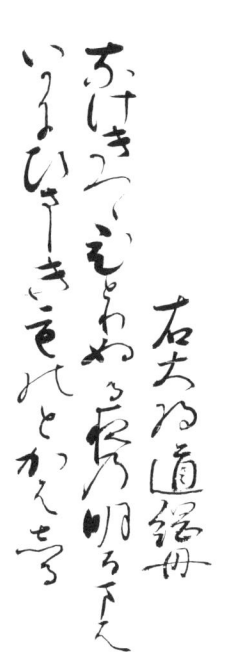

54. TAKAKO, MOTHER OF THE HONORARY GRAND MINISTER

You promise you
will never forget,
but to the end of time
is too long to ask.
So let me die today,
still loved by you.

55. FUJIWARA NO KINTŌ

The waterfall, dried up
in the distant past,
makes no sound at all,
but the fame
of the cascade
flows on and on,
can still be heard today.

56. IZUMI SHIKIBU

As I will soon be gone,
let me take one more memory
of this world with me.
I hope against hope
to see you one more time,
to see you *now*.

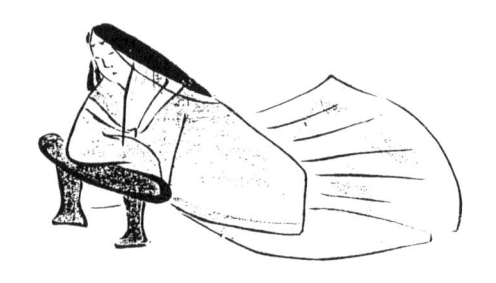

57. MURASAKI SHIKIBU

Was it you that I met
after all this time?
You were gone so quickly
like the midnight moon
disappearing behind clouds.

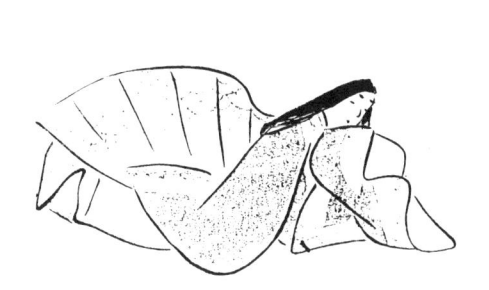

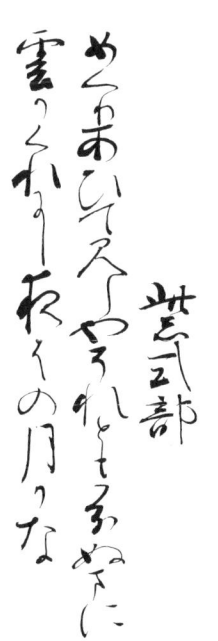

58. DAINI NO SANMI

At the foot of Mt. Arima
the wind rustles
through bamboo grasses
wavering yet constant—
the way my heart
beats only for you.

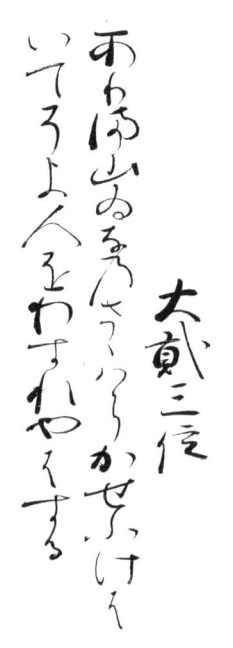

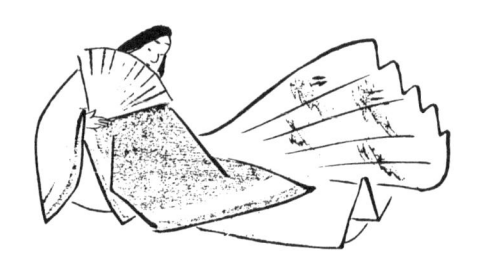

59. AKAZOME EMON

If I had known
you would not come
I could have gone to bed.
Instead I waited
through the deepening night,
but all that I got to meet
was the moon setting at dawn.

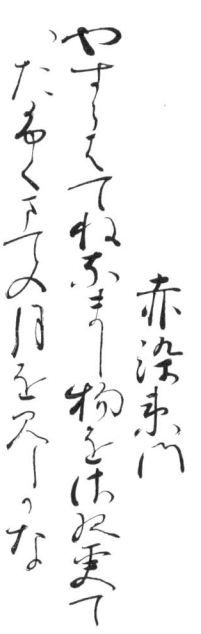

60. KOSHIKIBU

How could my mother
help me write this poem?
I have neither been
to Ōe Mountain nor Ikuno
nor have any letters
come from her
in a place so far away it's called—
The Bridge to Heaven.

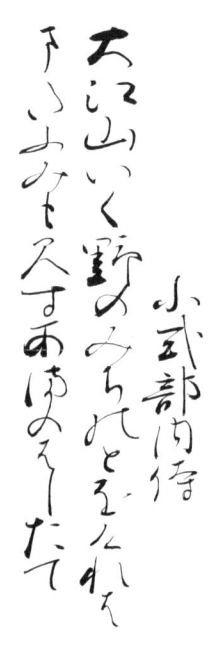

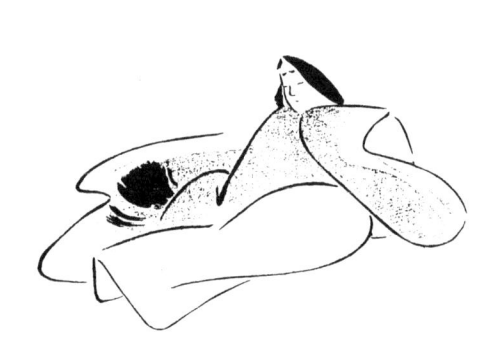

61. ISE NO TAIFU

The eightfold cherry blossoms
from Nara's ancient capital
bloom afresh today
in the new palace of Kyoto
with its nine splendid gates!

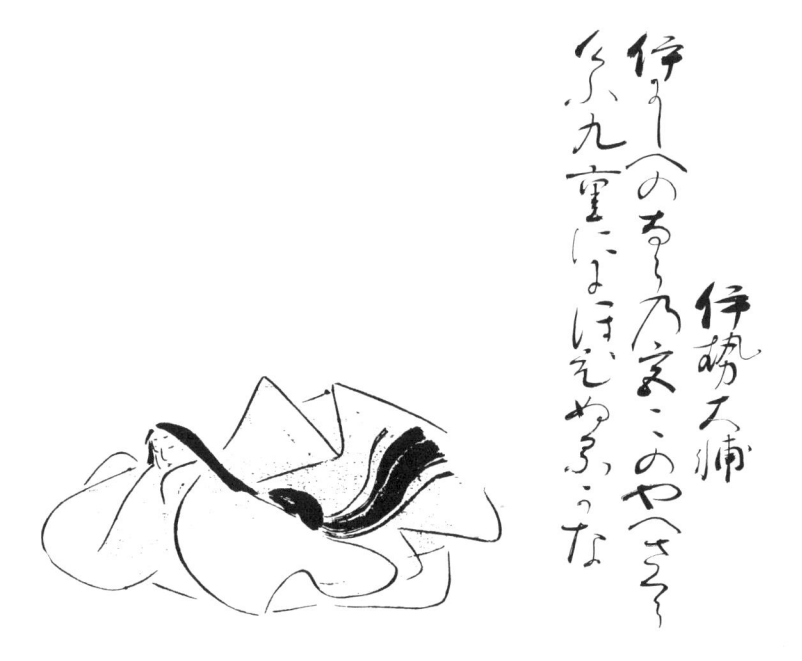

62. SEI SHŌNAGON

I am not deceived
by those who go home early
in the middle of the night,
falsely crowing like the cock
to pretend it's dawn.
May the barrier guards
of Meeting Hill
never let you through again.

63. FUJIWARA NO MICHIMASA

Because it is forbidden,
now all I can think of
is to find a way
to meet one last time.
Rather than your hearing it
from someone else,
I want to tell you myself—
we can never meet again!

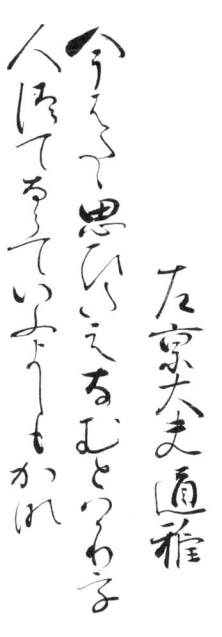

64. FUJIWARA NO SADAYORI

As the fog rises
and thins in patches,
in the shallows appear
stakes of the fishing nets—
Winter, dawn, the Uji river.

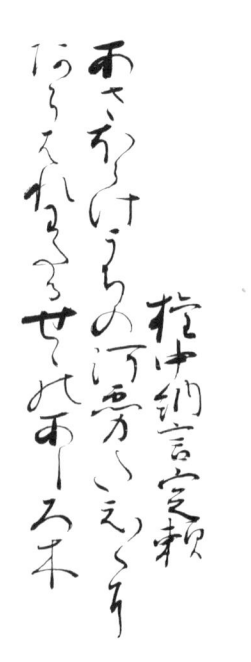

65. SAGAMI

My sleeves will never dry
with all these bitter tears
of unrequited love.
But even worse,
the regret of having lost
my good name—
tainted by this love.

66. PRELATE GYŌSON

Mountain cherry,
let us console each other.
Of all those I know
no one understands me
the way your blossoms do.

67. COURT HANDMAID SUŌ, NAKAKO

I would be sorry
to lose my good name
for laying my head
upon your arm
offered as a pillow
for a moment fleeting
as a spring night's dream.

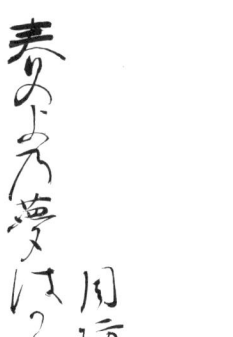

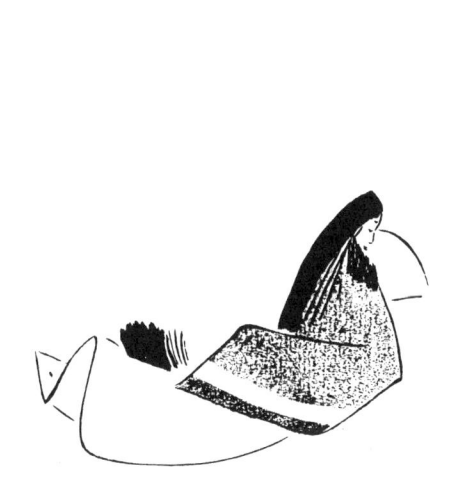

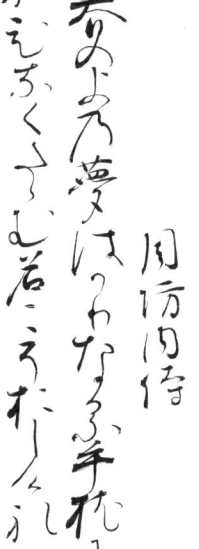

68. RETIRED EMPEROR SANJŌ

Though it's against my wish,
I must go on living
in this world of pain.
But from now on
I am sure I'll recall fondly
how bright the moon shone
at this hour of darkest night.

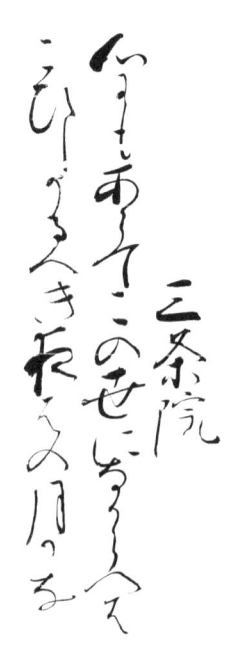

69. PRIEST NŌIN

Blown by storm winds,
Mt. Mimuro's autumn leaves
have become Tatsuta river's
richly hued brocade!

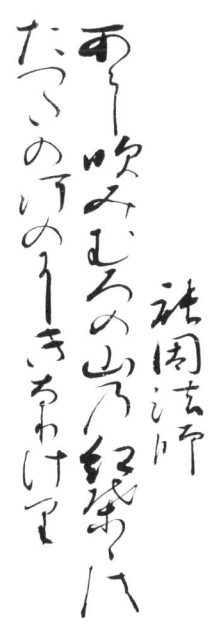

70. PRIEST RYŌZEN

Lonely, I step outside my hut
and look vacantly around:
It's the same all over—
Autumn dusk!

71. MINAMOTO NO TSUNENOBU

As evening draws near
in the field before the gate
the autumn wind rustles
in the ripened ears of rice
and the eaves of my reed hut.

72. LADY KII

I keep well away
from the well-known fickle waves
that pound on Takashi shore,
for I know I'd be sorry
if my sleeves got wet.

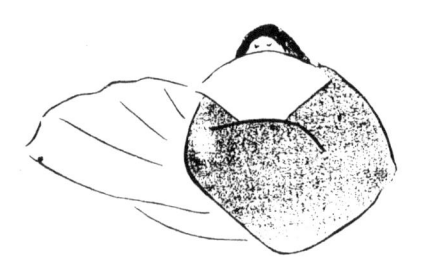

73. ŌE NO MASAFUSA

How lovely the cherry blossoms
blooming high on the mountain.
May the mists in the foothills
not rise and block the view.

74. MINAMOTO NO TOSHIYORI

At Hase I prayed to Kannon
to plead with her
who made me suffer so,
but like fierce storm winds
raging down the mountain
she became colder still—
It's not what I asked for...

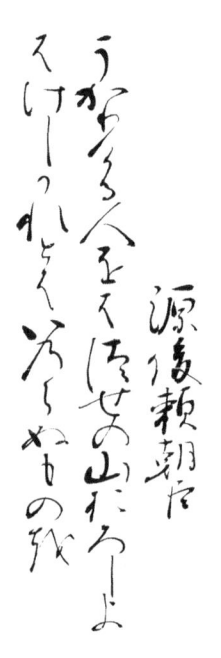

75. FUJIWARA NO MOTOTOSHI

I had been living on
for all those promises
like dew drops
on the *sasemo*.
Yet again this year
Autumn passes,
and they evaporate.

76. FUJIWARA NO TADAMICHI

When I row out
into the vast ocean
and look all around—
I cannot tell white billows
in the offing
from the far-off clouds.

77. RETIRED EMPEROR SUTOKU

Like water
rushing down
the river rapids,
we may be parted
by a rock,
but in the end
we will be one again.

78. MINAMOTO NO KANEMASA

Barrier guard of Suma:
How many nights
have you been wakened
by their sad lament—
the keening plovers
returning from Awaji?

79. FUJIWARA NO AKISUKE

Breezes blow long,
trailing clouds
across the sky
on this dark
autumn night.
Through breaks
the moon
so clear, so bright!

80. HORIKAWA

I do not know if you
will always be true.
This morning after you left,
I recalled your vows to me
looking at my long black hair
so disheveled—
like the tangles in my heart.

81. FUJIWARA NO SANESADA

I look out to where
the little cuckoo called,
but all that's left
is a pale moon
in the dawn sky.

82. PRIEST DŌIN

Despite this suffering
I somehow stay alive
yet with all this pain
of loving you
I cannot stop my sadness
nor the tears that flow.

83. FUJIWARA NO TOSHINARI

There is no way
to escape the world.
My mind made up
I have entered
deep in the mountains,
but even here
my pain is echoed
in the plaintive belling
of the stag.

84. FUJIWARA NO KIYOSUKE

If I live long,
I may look back
with yearning
for these painful days—
the world that now
seems harsh
may then appear
sweet and good!

85. PRIEST SHUN'E

The only relief from the pain
of waiting all night long
for a lover who does not come
would be the break of day,
but even gaps in the shutters
are too cruel to let in the light of dawn.

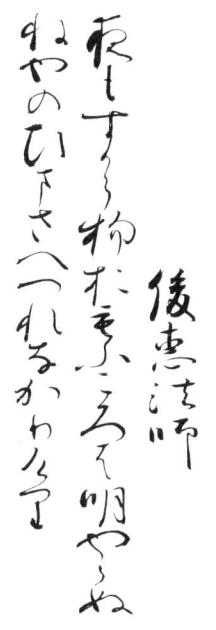

86. PRIEST SAIGYŌ

As if it were the moon
that bids me grieve
I look up and try
to blame her.
But in my heart
I know full well
these bitter tears
flow down my face
for someone else.

87. PRIEST JAKUREN

The drops from a light shower
have not yet dried
on the leaves of the black pines
before wisps of fog rise
in the autumn dusk.

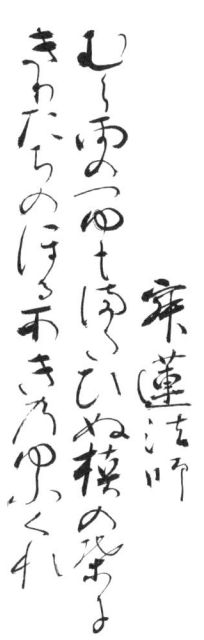

88. KŌKAMON IN NO BETTŌ

For the sake of one night
on Naniwa Bay
short as the nodes
of a reed cut at the root
what is left for me?
Like the wooden
channel markers
out in the sea
must I, too,
wear myself out
pining for my love?

89. PRINCESS SHOKUSHI

If I live longer I cannot bear
to hide this secret love.
Jeweled thread of life
since you must break—
let it be now

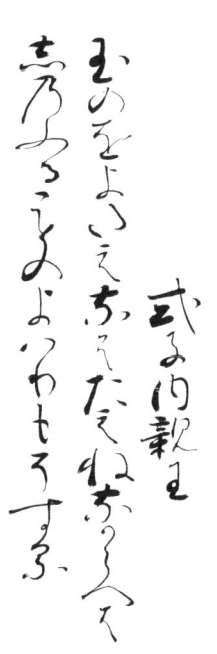

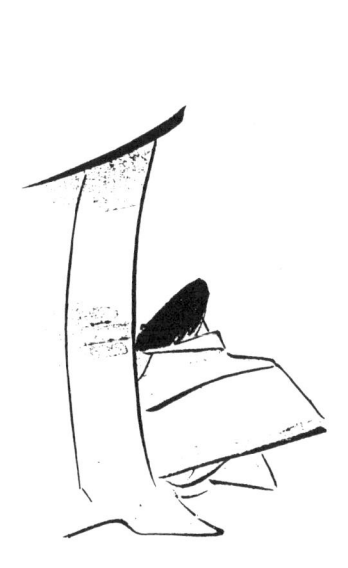

90. INPUMON IN NO TAIFU

How I'd to like to show him!
The fishermen's sleeves of Ojima
are drenched indeed
but even so
they have not changed color
like mine bathed in tears.

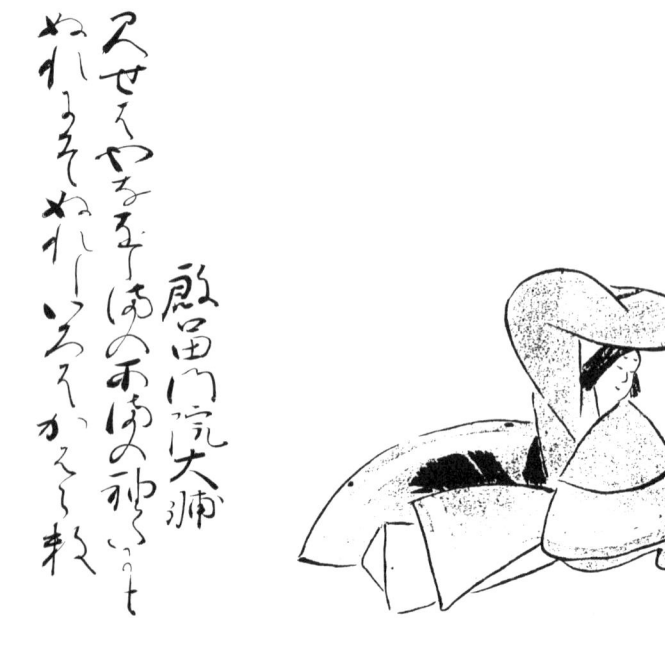

91. FUJIWARA NO YOSHITSUNE

The crickets cry
on this frosty night
as I spread my robe for one
on the cold straw mat.
Must I sleep alone?

92. LADY SANUKI

My sleeves are like rocks
far out into the sea.
Even at low tide
they cannot be seen
by anyone,
nor will they ever dry.

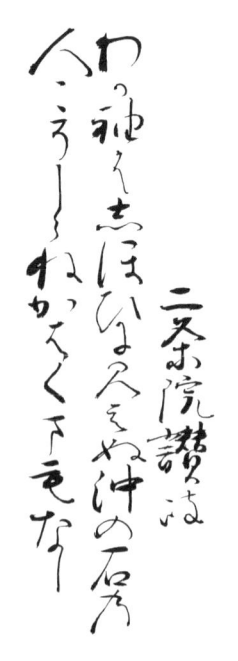

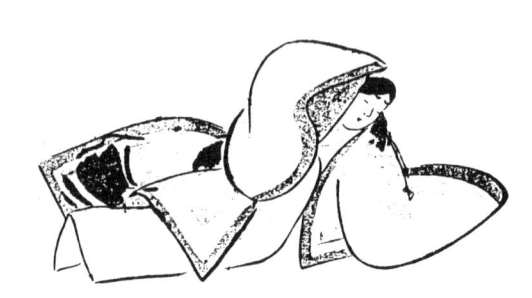

93. MINAMOTO NO SANETOMO

Would that things not change.
These simple moving sights—
Fishermen at their common chores,
rowing their small boats,
pulling nets along the shore.

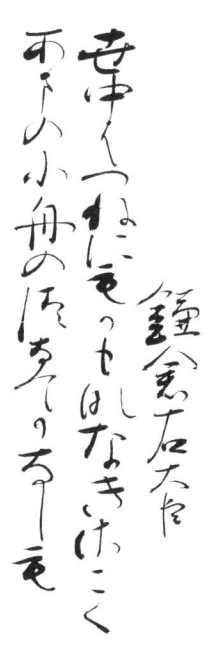

94. FUJIWARA NO MASATSUNE

The autumn wind
blowing down
the mountain
brings on the night.
At the old capital
of Yoshino
it gets colder,
and I can hear
pounding—
cloth being fulled.

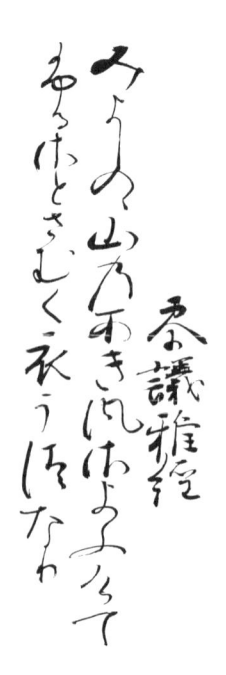

95. EX HIGH PRELATE JIEN

Though not good enough
for the good of the people,
as I have begun to live here
in this timber forest,
I would protect them
with these ink-black robes
of the Buddha's Way.

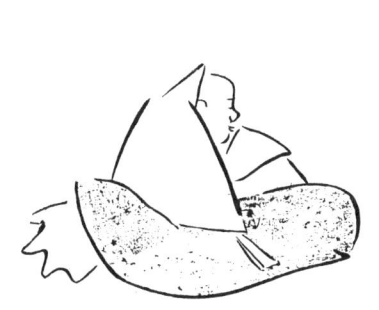

96. FUJIWARA NO KINTSUNE

As if lured by the storm
the blossoms are strewn about
white upon the garden floor,
yet all this whiteness is not snow—
rather, it is me
who withers and grows old.

97. FUJIWARA NO TEIKA

On the shore of Matsuo Bay
waiting for you
who do not come
my heart burns
like the flames
of salt-making fires
burning fiercely
in the evening calm.

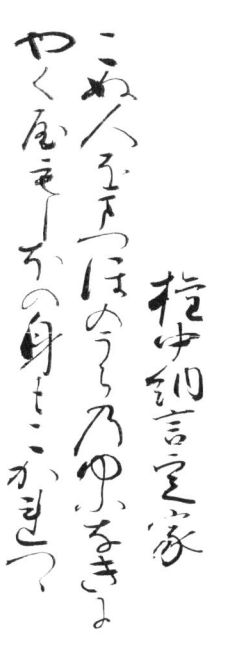

98. FUJIWARA NO IETAKA

Twilight. A chill wind rustles
over the little river
lined with oak trees.
End of season cleansing rites
are the only sign
we're still in summer.

99. GOTOBA IN

In spite of myself
I spend so much time
brooding over things—
There are some I love,
some I hate,
and even times
when I hate
the very ones I love.

100. JUNTOKU IN

Memory ferns sprout in the eaves
of the old forsaken palace.
But however much I long for them,
they never will come back—
the days of old.

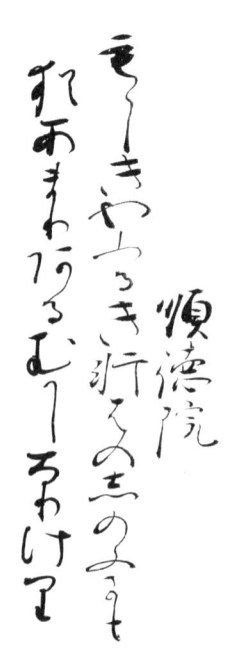

APPENDIX

The Colors of the Flower: Poem 9 as an Example of
Code Language and Multiplicity of Meanings in *Waka*

Many people have written of this poem as a *cri de coeur* of an old woman who in her heyday was a very great beauty, blessed with exceptional talent, sensually alive, and feted and loved by many. Now she is withered, her beauty gone, her friends and lovers dead or having forgotten her, her sensuality drained, her mind deteriorating, her poetic talent impaired, a miserable ruin of what she once was.

I do not disagree with this interpretation, but additional considerations must also be taken into account. The most striking feature of the poem is that it is a masterpiece. Almost every word is embroidered with many layers of meaning, creating an effect of rich emotional intensity and stunning intellectual prowess.

Ono no Komachi is like many superior Japanese women. In Japanese culture, women have traditionally been relegated to roles subservient to men, which has meant that they have had less freedom and greater challenges in expressing themselves. One of the principal modes of expression employed—and still practiced even today—was self-abnegation. In this poem, Ono no Komachi employs the classical rhetoric of self-abnegation in an ostensible lament for her fading beauty and talents.

It is true that she laments the loss of her youth, beauty and talents, but it is also true that she does so in a way that only a genius at the height of her powers could do. While completely self-effacing, she is at the same time self-affirming. It is difficult to imagine that she was unaware of her achievement. In other words, the poet is saying something like, "Yes, I am growing old and am less beautiful than I once was. Maybe you superficial (especially male!) readers will no longer find me beautiful, but if you have half a heart you will be able to see through my many-layered disguise and know that the sadness of life has sharpened my genius, and, while dissembling weakness, I have made up in mental ingenuity what I have lost in my physical prowess. I am diminished physically, perhaps, but I am still also at the peak of my creative powers. Fade away, those of you who can only see the surface, for you will surely take me only at the level of my words; but even those of you who can see beyond the surface, approach gingerly, for the profundity of my emotion has made me as formidable as ever."

Helen McCullough's exhaustive study of the *Kokin Wakashū*, *Brocade by Night: "Kokin Wakashū" and the Court Style in Japanese Classical Poetry* offers a longer discussion of Ono no Komachi's achievements. She notes in particular that "word association" (*engo*) is "capable not only of supplying wit but also of creating romantic, melancholy overtones, which were almost invariably achieved through the association of human feeling with the world of nature" (350).

The following is an example of the complexity of some poems in the *Hyakunin Isshu*, demonstrating multiple overlapping meanings. The Japanese text of poem 9 reads:

> hana no iro wa
> utsurinikeri na
> itazura ni

Appendix 107

wa ga mi yo ni furu
nagame seshi ma ni

The diverse meanings conveyed in the text comprise the following:

hana	flower, beauty, poetic or artistic talent.
Wa	more than the simple subject particle, it functions here as an extra syllable (*ji-amari*) charged with uncontainable, verbally inexpressible feeling. It is also a strong intensifier.
Iro	color, sexuality, or sensuality.
Utsuru	(dictionary form of *utsurinikeri*) to pale or fade, change, scatter.
Na	emphatic, expressing overwhelming emotion, a profound sigh of sorrow.
itazura ni	in vain, come to nothing, meaningless time passed by. The poem pivots on this line. Peerless beauty and youth and talent and love now seem all in vain. Then the poem pivots to "my (whole) life in vain." Thus, *itazura* modifies both what precedes and what follows it.
waga mi	my life.
waga mi yo ni	like my life.
waga mi yo ni furu	"My body grows old" and "as I passed the time away" (an idiom meaning something like "in idle chat").
Yo	world, life, sexual relations
yo ni furu	like, as.
Furu	to grow old, falling rain, to pass through life.
Nagame	be lost in thought, long rains, gaze out upon (as in the rains).
furu nagame	is the "endless-falling rain." The preceding phrase overlaps the following one: *nagame seshi ma ni*, "while I gaze at it"

"Hana no iro wa / Utsurinikeri na . . ." has three distinct meanings.

1. The literal meaning that the cherry blossoms are faded.
2. The metaphorical meaning that the beautiful woman's (*hana no*) charms, beauty, and sensuality (*iro*) are gone.
3. The metaphorical meaning that her superlative talent for good poetry (*hana*) has now deserted her.

Most critics have interpreted the long rains as those of spring, but according to another interpretation, the poem progresses metaphorically from youth to old age: it begins with spring, not mentioned but clearly evoked by the flowers (which for readers of classical Japanese invariably meant cherry blossoms), and ends with late autumn, not mentioned but clearly evoked by the long rains of that season. The evoked season of autumn is also a homonym for *aki* (fatigue, melancholy, or *taedium vitae*). It is interesting to note that at least one early illustration shows Komachi wearing a kimono with a maple-leaf design on it.

At its simplest level, it can be read simply as a poem describing the blossoms blooming in vain and scattering in the long rains. But it is unlikely that the poem is so superficial, because its other resonances are so rich and apparent. I have tried repeatedly to translate it into English in one short version but finally decided that it was impossible. It is impossible for an English-language translation to capture all the nuances in the original without becoming overloaded, yet because of the many exclusions necessary the translation conveys only part of the rich suggestive quality of the original. Not only is there the problem of translating all the rich innuendo and multiplicity of meaning, but there is also the problem of conveying that which is unsaid but so apparent: the undeniable affirmation of the poet's undiminished genius. This extraordinarily dense poem is brilliantly confined to thirty-two syllables in Japanese, an extra syllable being a code for emotion too great to express.

A translation like the one below, which attempts to encompass everything in the original, is no more than a list of the implied elements in the original and cannot be considered poetry:

> A life in vain.
> I've grown old
> so quickly—
> lovers gone,
> my beauty
> talents faded
> like these blossoms
> fading in endless rain
> that I sit here
> alone
> lost in thought
> gazing.

In the last few lines, what is expressed so suggestively in the original has become an overloaded litany, so the translation falls flat. Another alternative is to translate "alone/lost in thought" as "so sadly," as in the following:

> A life in vain.
> I've grown old
> my beauty
> talents faded
> like these blossoms
> fading in endless rain
> that I sit here so sadly
> gazing out upon.

The poem is full of an intense sadness made all the more poignant because it is that of a genius preening her magnificent feathers while simultaneously lamenting the passing of her youth. Although "so sadly" works well in this case, the great early Japanese poet and editor Ki no Tsurayuki says we must merely suggest emotions like sadness but not write them directly. I have read more than a dozen translations of this poem, dating from over a hundred years ago to the present, but have not read a single one that is completely satisfactory, though some are very good. The remaining choice is either to translate only part of the poem or to offer several versions. But even if it were possible to render all the nuances of what is said overtly in the original, one is still left with the task of translating what is inferred to great artistic effect. That version awaits the translator whose talents exceed my own.

AFTERWORD

It gives me particular satisfaction to see this new translation of the *Hyakunin Isshu*. This short collection of classic *waka* poems has been rendered into English many times already, and there are several versions in other European languages, too, but I have not yet read a satisfactory translation. Some versions are mere doggerel, whereas the originals are of extremely high quality. Some scholarly versions are very helpful, indeed, especially Joshua Mostow's impressive *Pictures of the Heart*, but he generously concedes that there will never be a definitive translation of the *Hyakunin Isshu*, and now Peter McMillan gives us a new version.

The hundred poets are among Japan's greatest. They knew everything that is known about lyric poetry. They wrote from the heart and spoke to the heart. The translator must have a very thorough knowledge of the Japanese language and its extraordinary resources. He must be a person of deep feeling, who can fully grasp the emotion of each poem and convey what he has felt as fully as possible in graceful English. McMillan, himself a poet, is admirably equipped for this task.

However, the task of translating these poets is daunting. The poets wrote in a hallowed tradition that had so many conventions and restricting rules applied in a very brief form that one wonders, as with the old bards of the Irish Gaelic tradition, how they could express any feeling at all. Yet these short but very great poems have extraordinary power.

Following are four lines of English lyric poetry, part of a long ballad but generally cited alone.

> Oh! Westron wind, when wilt thou blow
> That the small rain down can rain
> Christ, that my love were in my arms
> And we in bed again!

These first four lines move one in the way a great *waka* can.

Similarly, there is an Irish quatrain, piously ascribed to Grainne of the Finn Cycle of tales, though the language is more likely from the tenth century, long after her time, in which she is made to speak of the handsome Diarmait:

Fil duine	There is one
Frismad buide lemm diuterc,	I would gladly look upon,
Dia tibrinn in mbith mbuide,	For whom I'd give the gold world,
Huile, huile, cid diupert.	All, all, though it be my loss.

This *cri de coeur* also has the feel of a good *waka*. Translating it is extremely difficult, but in no way as daunting as trying to render classical Japanese poetry.

Of all the poems in the *Hyakunin Isshu*, perhaps the most difficult to translate is poem 9 by the female poet Ono no Komachi. Also during the ninth century, a great poem by a female poet on the same universal theme, the pity of aging, loss of youth, beauty, friends, lovers and poetic talent, was written in Irish Gaelic by someone known only as the Nun (or maybe Hag) of Beare. She uses thirty-four (some say thirty-five) stanzas of four lines each.

Komachi uses one *waka* of five lines and manages to convey the same thing. Her poem is a miracle of density, verbal music, resonance, rich in overtones and undertones, alluding to earlier poems in Japanese and also Chinese, resorting to age-old convention, but making it fresh ("make it new" was a rule in composing *waka*; Ezra Pound gets too much credit for inventing this slogan). A full translation of all that Komachi manages to say in thirty-two syllables could take ten stanzas in English.

In this light, one might take issue with the atypically misleading judgment of the great Arthur Waley on the *Hyakunin Isshu*, namely, that it displays the least pleasing features of Japanese poetry. According to Waley:

> Artificialities of every kind abound, and the choice does little credit to the taste of Sadaiye [Teika] to whom the compilation is attributed. These poems have gained an unmerited circulation in Japan, owing to the fact that they are used in a kind of "Happy Families" card game. (*Japanese Poetry*, 7)

In fact, the reverse is true. It has provided much of the *éducation sentimentale* as well as the literary inspiration for the Japanese over seven centuries.

Peter McMillan is very conscious of the exceptional quality of this collection. He might have tried to stay closer to the stanza form, as I always despairingly try to do myself, but he has decided—wisely, I concede—to use a very free form, rather than do violence to language and force the poems in English into an uncomfortable straitjacket. This translation for the general reader has been a labor of love. The *Hyakunin Isshu* is one of the best keys to the mentality and spirit of the Japanese. I am happy at last to see it available in this unpretentious, reliable, and satisfyingly poetic translation.

Eileen Kato

Figure 3. Hyakunin Isshu *playing cards from the middle Edo period. Woodblock print with hand-painting. Calligraphy by hand. (Collection of Hideji Ōyagi) Photographs by Yukiko Hirota.*

NOTES ON THE POEMS

1. This poem reads most effectively as a love poem, so I have left the translation open to both readings. The unnamed but clear reference to tears in the use of the established convention of wet sleeves could be both for a loved one or for the populace in general, so this poem has been interpreted in different ways. A common interpretation is as a love poem, but the one Teika is said to have preferred was that of a caring emperor crying in sympathy for the hardship of his people—thus making it appropriate to open this collection. However, if it is read together with poems 2 and 3, one can see that the dampened sleeves of the emperor and Hitomaro are being symbolically hung out to dry by the daughter empress whose reign is depicted as being full of brightness and light.
2. Jitō was a female Emperor. Mount Kagu is the location of the stone door behind which the Sun Goddess and mythical progenitrix of the divine imperial line, Amaterasu, retreated, plunging the world temporarily into darkness. In the poem, all is white and light and highly auspicious, suggesting the blessing of Amaterasu. The poem makes an obvious link between the light of the Sun Goddess and the benevolent rule of the emperor, her earthly descendent. Mount Kagu was also used metaphorically in poems to celebrate the longevity of an emperor and was one of the three Nara hills sung about in a *chōka*

by her father in the *Man'yōshū*. This poem, written by the daughter of the author of poem 1, Emperor Tenji, emphasizes the hereditary nature of both imperial rule and poetic craft. The importance of heredity is also echoed in the selection of poems 99 and 100, by the Emperor GoToba and his son Juntoku. In Japanese, the line *ama no kagu yama* means a "mountain of the skies," which I have translated as "beloved of the gods." This poem expressing surprise at season change is echoed in poem 98, which also expresses surprise at season change. In this poem Emperor Jitō, upon seeing the summer robes on Mount Kagu, realizes that spring has already passed, and in poem 98 Ietaka realizes that, even though the air has become chilly, it is still summer.

3. The poem plays on the great length of the copper pheasant's tail, the long night spent alone, and a belief that the male and female pheasant parted from each other at night and slept in separate valleys. The layout is meant to convey visually the long night and the long tail.

5. In this poem, the subject is unclear, so it could be either the deer or the poet who is going deeper into the mountains. I have translated it with a human subject and given a more ambiguous rendering similar to the original as follows: "How forlorn the autumn. / Rustling through the piled up leaves / and moving on alone / into the deep mountain—/ the plaintive belling of the stag."

6. This poem has two distinct interpretations. One interprets the Bridge of Magpie Wings as the Milky Way spread across the sky, enabling the Ox Boy to make his yearly visit to his beloved, the Weaving Maid, in a Chinese tale known in Japan as the Tanabata, these days celebrated every year on July 7. In the old calendar, however, the Tanabata was celebrated on the seventh day of the seventh month, which would be sometime in August. It is important to point this out as July 7 is still in the rainy season in Japan. As it very often rains on this day, it would be difficult for the Herd Boy to make his journey across the sky, unlike the clear weather of high summer of the date of the lunar calendar. The version above follows the second interpretation, namely, that the magpie bridge refers to bridges or stairs leading to the palace, especially the passageways that lovers used for secret meetings. In other words, this is an

example of *mitateru*, a metaphorical comparison in which one sees one thing in terms of something else. In this poem, the poet plays on the homonym for "bridge" and "stairs" and thereby infers that the imperial palace is also a heavenly world like the world of the magpie bridge in the sky. The white ribbon could refer both to the frost and the white in the magpies' wings. In this version, stairs or bridges in the palace turn a brilliant white when covered with frost. In classical Japanese, and even to some extent today, the court was known as the *kumo no ue* (Above the Clouds), and the courtiers who live above the clouds (*kumo no uebito*).

7. Nakamaro was sent to study in China for many years and finally got a chance to return home. He is said to have composed this poem on the night of his farewell party, recalling the moon rising over Kasuga Shrine, where he had gone to pray before he left Japan. Kasuga Shrine was where the Japanese went to pray for a safe return before leaving the country, so the poem is filled with poignancy and irony because Nakamaro's ship was shipwrecked on the way back, and he never returned to Japan. The mention of "Kasuga" is also a poetic convention for such invocations before departure.

8. Mount Uji. "Uji" refers to the Uji river, and Mount Uji became associated with sorrow. The poem plays on the homonym *u* as in Uji, which means "sorrow." Interpretations of the poem vary. Some see the poet agreeing with the general view of Uji as a sad place, but others see the poet as living happily in Uji.

10. The Osaka Barrier is east of Kyoto. The "au" of Ausaka (another reading for this word) is a homonym for "to meet."

11. According to the headnote in the *Kokinshū*, this poem was sent to someone in the capital as Takamura was being sent into exile on the island of Oki. Takamura was sent into exile for refusing to join the mission to China in 838 but was pardoned a year later. There is another interpretation of this poem wherein the poet asks the boats to tell his beloved of his exile: "Boats of the fishermen / tell her, please, / I'm being rowed away to exile / through the myriad islets/ to the great ocean beyond."

12. According to the headnote in the *Kokinshū*, the poem was composed

after seeing the Gosechi dancers. The dance celebrates the harvest in the eleventh month and was performed by young maidens of the nobility. The dance was believed to have originated with Emperor Tenmu (r. 673–686) when he was visiting Mount Yoshino. When night fell, and the emperor played on his koto, heavenly dancers appeared in the sky. The poet, by suggesting that the real dancers before his eyes are like the heavenly ones, implicitly elevates the reign of Ninmyō to that of the great Tenmu.

13. According to the headnote in the *Gosenshū*, this poem was sent to Princess Suishi (Yasuko), who later entered the household of Yōzei. Yōzei was the father of Prince Motoyoshi (poem 20), so this is another example of Teika affirming the importance of imperial rule and the practice of *waka* poetry.

14. This poem contains a good example of the complexity of meanings one word can have in classical Japanese. *Shinobu* in the poem is a hill and the place name of an area; it also means "to love secretly." In addition, it is also a kind of fern, perhaps like the *spiranthes australis* (some say it is closer to the *davallia mariesii*) and the name of a cloth that tears easily, like the fragile love being described. The pattern described in the poem was made by placing fabric over ferns spread out on a large rock and then beating on the fabric with a stone or rock to make the disordered patterns. Another theory suggests that the ferns were placed on top of the fabric and then beaten into it. A great rock where such fabric was dyed can still be seen today near Fukushima city and was described by Bashō in his *Oku no Hosomichi* (Narrow Road to the North). The poet is the protagonist of one of the most famous of Nō plays, *Tōru*, attributed to Zeami.

15. The greens referred to in the poem are the seven herbs and vegetables eaten at the beginning of spring.

seri	water dropwort (Japanese parsley)
nazuna	shepherd's purse
gogyō	cudweed
hakobera	chickweed
hotoke-no-za	nipplewort (henbit)

suzuna (kabu)	Japanese turnip (Chinese rape)
suzushiro	*daikon* radish (*raphanus sativus*); garden cress (*arabis flagellosa*)

Plants are generally listed only by their English names, but where the English name does not correspond closely to the actual plant the Latin names are also indicated. In the above list sometimes two plants have the same name, so I have given precedence to the name as used when referring to one of the seven plants. The Festival of the Seven Herbs (*nanakusa no sekku*) on January 7 is an ancient tradition in Japan when rice porridge is eaten with seven vegetables and herbs.

16. Inaba is both a place name and a verb form meaning "if I leave." The Japanese word *matsu* is the only word I know of that has the same two meanings in English and in Japanese, namely, "pine tree" and "to pine" for someone. It is a bit overdone in English to pun on "pine" with both meanings, but I use it because it is the only example that illustrates exactly the kind of wordplay that is common in Japanese. The original does not have the expression "famous for," but the mention of Inaba would conjure up the famous pines for Japanese readers of that period, so it is a justifiable addition.
17. The original meaning of the poem as it appeared in the *Kokinshū* was *mizu kukuru* meaning "tie-dyed water," a reading that supports the use of "brocade" in the main translation, but Teika may have read it as *mizu kuguru*, meaning "water flowing under" (with leaves floating on the surface) as follows.

> Even the almighty
> gods of old
> never knew
> such beauty:
> The Tatsuta river
> in autumn sunlight—
> reds flowing above,
>
> the water below.

In classical Japanese kana, the possibility of reading the word *kukuru* either as *kukuru* or as *kuguru* is a good example of the way in which ambiguity in orthography contributed to poetic polysemy. I have generally followed Teika's readings of the poems, but in the case above I put the *Kokinshū* version in the main text.

18. It was believed that those who were deeply in love visited their lovers in dreams. There is an alternative version of this poem in which it is the poet who has lost confidence and will not visit the object of his love.

19. Formerly, in Japanese as in English, a "short space" could refer both to distance or time. Nowadays, in English the double meaning could cause confusion, but I decided to honor the older usage as it is the only way to integrate the metaphor introduced in the first part of the poem with that of the latter part.

20. The verb *mi o tsukusu*, which means "complete devotion" or "to give up everything for the sake of something," and this puns on the word for "channel markers" (*miotsukushi*) in the poem. The *miotsukushi* channel marker is on the present-day banners for the city of Osaka, symbolizing that those who work there exert all their energy in the service of the citizens of the city. The translation of the phrase as "self-sacrifice" is slightly extreme, but it works in the context of the poem. The interpretation by Teika and others may have been that it was not that he would risk his life but that she would not risk her name to see him. This poem is said to have been sent to Fujiwara no Hōshi after her affair with Motoyoshi became public knowledge. Fujiwara no Hōshi was at the time in the service of the Retired Emperor Uda, to whom she bore three sons. One can imagine that the scandal must have been considerable.

21. In the old calendar *nagatsuki* refers to the ninth month, the last month of autumn. It was quite common for poets to imagine themselves in the situation of others. In this case, a man imagines himself in the place of the woman who was waiting for a lover who did not come. An interpretation of this poem with a reading of the persona of the woman waiting for long nights instead of one night is also possible. "I'm coming right away" was presumably expressed only

once, and the pale moon is not necessarily seen at every dawn, thus inferring a specific sighting. Mostow mentions that Teika wrote a collection of commentaries on the *Kokinshū* called the *Kenchū Mikkan* in 1221. Judging from this, it seems likely that Teika read the poem as meaning many nights, perhaps because the longer duration created a narrative more consistent with his *yōen* aesthetic.

22. This *waka* plays on the idea that the Chinese ideograph for "storm" (*arashi*: 嵐) is made up of the character for "mountain" (*yama*: 山) above the character for "wind" (*kaze*: 風). Therefore it is natural that mountain winds should be called storms. The wit lies in the punning of the word *arashi* (storm) with the word *arasu* (to wrack or destroy). These kinds of witty interpretations were based on Chinese court-style poetry of the Six Dynasties (220–581), but it was not to the taste of Teika and others, who required a more serious emotional base for *waka*. One may reasonably presume that Teika and later readers rejected the original conception of the poem and read it as an atmospheric poem about the desolate feeling associated with a windswept autumn landscape as expressed in the version above. A more literal version, closer to the Chinese interpretation, would be something like: "The mountain wind / has just to blow / and the leaves and grasses of autumn / wither and die. / So that is why the elements / "wracking," "mountain," "wind" / make up the word for "storm."

25. The poem plays on the homonyms of several Japanese words. *Sanekazura* means "vine" but also "to spend the night together" as in "sleeping together." Meeting Hill, or Osaka, is both the "Meeting Slope" and a romantic encounter. It was customary for aristocratic men and women to live separately and for the men to visit the women, but commentators of the medieval period interpreted this poem to mean that the poet wished to draw his beloved to his own residence as if drawing in a piece of vine. Perhaps Sadakata attached an actual piece of vine to the *waka* when he sent it to his lady.

26. The imperial family and court members were great nature lovers then as now, and it was common practice to go on outings to enjoy scenic views of cherry blossoms or autumn foliage. In this poem,

Teika affirms the importance of regular imperial outings in the company of poets. These poets were also often the descendents of poets, so Teika is affirming both imperial and literary lineage. The purpose of the outings was not only to enjoy the beauties of nature but also to write poems about what they saw. Edward Kamens suggests that Teika is expressing loyalty to the disenfranchised imperial family (Wheelwright, *Word in Flower*, 26). Despite Teika's approval of such outings, he was angry at always having to accompany Emperor GoToba, as he had to pay his own expenses, and it meant he had to be away from home for several days at a time. He disapproved of the emperor's way of life, blaming it on the negative influence of his ministers, Teika's political enemies (Brower and Miner, *Fujiwara Teika's Superior Poems of Our Time*, 9).

28. Recently, it has become fashionable to discuss homosexuality in terms of Japanese classical literature. The openly lesbian feminist scholar of Japanese literature Komashaku Kimi, for example, writes on the topic of Murasaki Shikibu's lesbianism and her love for another lady-in-waiting, KoShōshō. Many Edo-period illustrations of the poems, especially some by the great early *ukiyo-e* artist Hishikawa Moronobu (c.1618–1694), depict homoerotic scenes. In Moronobu's picture of this poem, an older man looks longingly from under his bed coverings on a younger man. Illustrations of poems 35, 47, and 49 also depict such scenes, some no doubt influenced by Saikaku's homosexual novel *The Great Mirror of Male Love*. Mostow's introduction and accounts of the individual poems mentioned here have a fuller discussion of this theme.

29. This poem must have been one of Teika's favorites, as he included it in several compilations.

30. According to the *Kokon Chomonjū*, Inmei Mon'in (wife of the Emperor Tsuchimikado) asked Teika and Ietaka separately what they considered the best poem in the *Kokinshū*, and both responded: Tadamine's poem. The same story appears in Ichijou Kanera's *Dōmōshō* (a later work than the *Kokon Chomonjū*), in which the person asking the question was GoToba.

31. *Asaborake* means "dawn" but suggests an autumn or winter dawn.

32. The visual arrangement of the text is meant to recreate the image described in the poem. The blank space between lines 4 and 5 is meant to suggest how the leaves temporarily block the flow of the stream.
35. In classical Japanese, the plum is a symbol of fond remembrance of the past.
42. Mount Forever is a translation of Sue no Matsu Yama (Mt. Sue), which means the mountain that lasts until the end of time. This poem also refers to the *Kokinshū* poem: "Kimi wo okite / adashi gokoro wo / ware moteba / sue no matsu yama / nami mo kosanan" (Should I be unfaithful / and leave you / may the waves rise / and swallow up the pines of Mount Forever). The idea is that because Mt. Sue was so high, it would be impossible for the waves to rise high enough to swallow them, just as it would be for the poet to be unfaithful.
51. Moxa: The moxa plant (*artemesia vulgari*) is used as a natural remedy, for example, in moxibustion, that is, heating or burning certain areas of the body by applying a pad made of the powdered leaves of the moxa plant.
52. According to the headnote in the *Goshūishū*, this poem was composed while the poet was on his way home, as falling snow was piling up on the pathway.
55. According to the headnote in the *Shūishū*, this poem is about an old waterfall in Daikakuji. However, the location that I visited in Daikakuji commemorating this poem resembles a dried-up spring more than a waterfall.
60. Koshikibu no Naishi wrote this poem, one of the most brilliant in the collection, in response to being teased that she could not write a poem without the help of her mother, the famous poet Izumi Shikibu. It is a devastating retort, full of puns and word association, that also conveys the great distance between mother and daughter by mentioning no fewer than three place names in a short *waka*. All three of these places must be passed through to get to the mother's house. Ama no Hashidate is one of them; it literally means the Bridge of Heaven, but I have translated it here as a Bridge to Heaven

to convey the sense of distance between the poet and her mother. In olden times and even today, Ama no Hashidate is one of the most famous scenic spots in Japan.

61. According to Ise no Tayū's *Collected Poems*, an eight-petaled cherry blossom was presented to the court by a bishop from Nara. The famous poet Murasaki Shikibu deferred to Ise no Tayū, who then accepted the blossom. Thereupon the great Michinaga insisted that a poem be written, so Ise no Tayū dashed off this stunning impromptu poem and thereby proved her genius. In classical Japanese, eightfold is a code for splendid and ninefold for something surpassing even the eightfold. Kyoto is often referred to in classical literature as *kokonoe no miyako*, the capital of nine gates. *Kokonoe*, or nine-layered, also refers to the court. The poem thus pays compliment to Michinaga and his daughter, the then-reigning empress. The *yae zakura* (eightfold cherry blossom) is a late-blooming variety for which Nara is famous.

62. This brilliant and witty poem first appeared in *The Pillow Book* by the same author and refers to a Chinese tale of the Lord of Mengchang, who escaped through the barrier of Hangu by imitating the sound of a cock crowing, so the guards, thinking it was dawn, opened the gates. The poet here refers to an incident when her lover, having to go home early, also imitated the sound of a cock crowing and wrote her a note the next day that he had wanted to stay longer, but the cock's crowing had forced him to leave. The poet's point is that even if the Chinese guards could be fooled, she was not. Meeting Hill is a translation of Osaka no Seki, the famous barrier that appears in several *waka* in this collection. The poet is also punning on the name of the barrier and the verb "to meet," especially the meeting of lovers. The poem is an example of the clever wit of the court ladies and of this one in particular.

66. In this *waka* "aware" can be interpreted as either "compassion" or "to console." Both are quite different in English, so an alternate version reads: "Mountain cherry, / let us have compassion for each other. / Of all those I know / no one understands me / as your blossoms do."

67. The headnote in the *Senzaishū* explains that on a spring night a group of people were chatting when the author reclined and said, "I wish I had a pillow." The Middle Counselor Tada'ie was eavesdropping on the conversation from behind the blinds and pushed his arm under them, saying, "Please use this as a pillow." The author replied with this romantic and playful lyric. *Haru no yo no yume* (spring night's dream) is a classical convention for something fleeting, such as a spring night's dream.

72. This poem was written as a negative response to a love poem in a Love Letter Competition (*kesō-bumi awase*) held in 1102. "To get wet" means not only from the waves but also from tears. The verb *nureru* means not only "to get wet (with the waves)" and "to cry" but also hints at love-making, and the implication of such a danger is embedded within the poem.

74. Lovers frequently visited Hase Temple to pray to the bodhisattva of compassion, Kannon. Some versions of the text do not have *yo* (*yamaoroshi yo*). However, in the *Senzaishū*, where the poem originally appears, and in a number of Teika texts as well as quite a few versions of the *Hyakunin Isshu* (including the calligraphic text used for this volume), it includes *yo*. Following Teika, I included it in the transliteration and Japanese versions, even though Shimazu does not have it.

75. The headnote in the *Senzaishū* for this poem states that Bishop Kōkaku's repeated requests to be made a lecturer for the Vimalakirti ceremony were overlooked, so his father appealed to the former chancellor Tadamichi. Tadamichi replied that he should be relied on to help the son by quoting a poem attributed to Kannon, bodhisattva of compassion, which states that the bodhisattva will provide salvation as long as there are *sasemo* plants growing on the plain of Shimeji (i.e., forever). That is why Bishop Kōkaku's father invokes the *sasemo* (moxa plant) in his bitter reply. The dew was a symbol of transience in classical Japanese, and here alludes to the transient nature of the promises.

78. In Japanese Awaji is a place name but also means "not to meet," and thus is a reason for the sad keening. The poem also alludes to the

chapter of *The Tale of Genji* in which Genji spends his exile in Suma near Awaji.

79. A more literal translation for *tsuki no kage* would be "moonlight," but that word already encompasses the notion of brightness, so to avoid repetition I translated it simply as "moon."

81. *Hototogisu* is the little cuckoo, in the same family as the cuckoo (*kakko*), and has a distinct call. Traditionally—but not in this poem—it is seen as a messenger from the dead.

82. A more literal translation is that although he can control his own emotions, his tears cannot and therefore flow involuntarily, as in the following translation: "Despite this suffering / I somehow stay alive, / yet unable to bear this pain / the helpless tears flow."

88. Naniwa Bay was a place that was famous for meeting pleasure girls. The channel markers that appear in several poems were made of wood and decayed quickly in the saltwater. Poem 19 also invokes the much-quoted symbol of a short time span, the reeds of Naniwa.

89. The word *tama* means both "jewel" and "soul." The jeweled thread of life was a metaphor for life itself.

90. The "him" in the first line refers to the poet Minamoto no Shigeyuki (poem 48), who wrote the original poem on which this is based, in which he simply states that both the sleeves of the fishermen and his own sleeves must be soaking wet. This poem develops the image further by saying that not only are the poet's sleeves soaked but they have also turned red because she has been crying tears of blood. The convention plays on the idea that both tears and seawater are made of saltwater. To have "wet sleeves" was a convention for "crying profusely from a broken heart." Crying "tears of blood" was a convention for "expressing deep suffering." As blood is only inferred in the original, I left it out in the translation, but it means that the dyeing that occurs is merely from tears.

91. The poet's robe was spread out as a coverlet and slept under.

93. This simple poem on the seascape off Kamakura telling of the poet's desire for an unchanging world has additional poignancy for readers who know that the poet was assassinated in Kamakura when he was only twenty-eight. Sanetomo studied poetry under Teika,

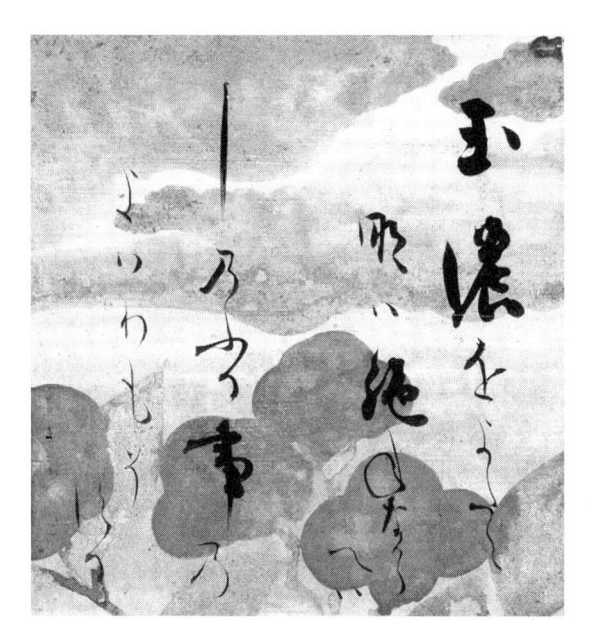

Figure 4. Tsubaki ni yuki zu. *Poem* (Shin Kokin Wakashū, no. 1034) (89 in the Hyakunin Isshu *but with slight variations in the text*). *Square paper* (shikishi) *with ground painting of camellia covered with snow, by Hon'ami Kōetsu. Painting attributed to Tawaraya Sōtatsu. From the* Shikishijo, *an album of poems from the* Shin Kokin Wakashū. *Calligraphy by Hon'ami Kōetsu (d. c. 1640). 36 leaves in total. Ink and color on paper, Edo period (seventeenth century).* (Gotoh Museum)

who gave him his *Kindai Shūka* (Superior Poems of Our Times) as a textbook.

94. "Fulling," the beating of cloth to make it smooth and bring out a sheen, is the antecedent of the domestic iron. *Furusato* can be translated as "the old capital" or as "my old home." In this poem it is generally understood to refer to the old capital, but it could also be interpreted as in the following translation. This alternate interpretation resonates more with the notion of an absent husband's hearing the cloth being fulled and feeling nostalgic for his wife and

home in the Chinese antecedent: "Wind blowing down / from the mountain / brings on the autumn night. / At my old home in Yoshino / it gets colder, / and I can hear the pounding / of cloth being fulled."

Teika wrote that the incorporation of earlier Chinese poems in the writing of *waka* should be used very selectively but that sometimes they can add an ingenious element to *waka*. This poem has both Chinese and Japanese antecedents. In the Chinese poem Li Bo describes the autumn atmosphere in terms of the sound of the fulling mallet beating cloth, an image in Chinese classical poetry connoting an absent husband recalling his beloved wife at home.

As to Japanese antecedents, Korenori's poem 325 in the *Kokinshū* describes Yoshino getting colder when the snow piles up in winter: "Mi-yoshino no / yama ni shirayuki / tsumoru rashi / furusato samuku / narimasaru keri" (It gets colder and colder / here in the home of my ancestors. / Snow must be piling up deeply / on Mt. Yoshino). In Masatsune's adaptation of this poem, the poet expresses a similar image of coldness but changes the season from winter to autumn and from falling snow to the soft sound of cloth being fulled at dusk. Thus one could see this poem as a superimposition of a classical Chinese poem upon a Japanese one to create a new poetic synthesis. Teika also advocated that, in adapting lines or images from earlier verse, one should change the subject matter. Thus this poem is a model of his poetic doctrine and a suitable model for the aspiring poet.

There is also a Chinese legend concerning Su Wu, who in ancient times was held in captivity by the Mongols. At night, he thought that he heard the sound of his wife's fulling mallet. He wrote her a letter and had it delivered by a wild goose. Upon receiving the letter, she told the emperor, who thereupon rescued Su Wu. A ballad is still sung today about this tale.

95. Mt. Hiei, which is inferred in the poem by mention of a forest, is the location of the central temple of the Tendai sect of Buddhism outside Kyoto. The poet is writing of his becoming a monk or joining a monastery.

97. Salt and salt-making connote bitterness and tears. Brine and seaweed were brought up from the sea in carts and boiled down on the shore to make salt.
98. This poem echoes poem 2, as both express surprise at the changing of the seasons. See poem 2 for another poem on season change. Generally, I have made a point of retaining Japanese place names, but in this case, I have translated and adapted the charming place name of Little River of the Oak Trees.
100. The standard translation for *Shinobu-gusa* is "hare's foot fern," but the word also puns on "remembering nostalgically." Thus the literal translation could be "remembering grass" or "memory ferns." This poem can be interpreted both as Juntoku's lament over the decline of imperial government and as Teika's own personal thoughts about the great poetry of the past or as both.

Figure 5. Hyakunin Isshu *playing cards. (Collection of Hideji Ōyagi)*

NOTES ON THE POETS

Because of discrepancy among the various sources for lifespan dates of the poets, some of the dates are approximate. In these notes, the term "entered religion" is used often. It covers a broad variety of meanings including being ordered to enter religion, entering religion as a necessity of being widowed, having a religious conversion, or joining a religious order.

1. Emperor Tenji, the thirty-eighth emperor (626–671; r. 668–671). He was the son of Jōmei and Kyōgoku (later named Saimei and twice a female emperor). Tenji vanquished the Soga clan with the help of Nakatomi no Kamatari, on whom he bestowed the family name Fujiwara in 669. He was especially revered by all the Fujiwara, including, of course, Teika. He built a palace on the shores of Lake Biwa, near present-day Ōtsu, and was deified and enshrined at Ōmi Jinja, which became closely associated with the *Hyakunin Isshu*. There has been and still is much controversy over the attribution of this poem to an emperor. The main reason for that is that the poem is found almost verbatim in the *Man'yōshū* with an anonymous attribution. However, the emperor depicted as a rice farmer was not incongruous to Japanese readers. Tenji is seen as the first reliably recorded progenitor of the imperial line and as the initiator of the close links between the court and poetry, links that survive to this day. There

are two *chōka* and four *tanka* attributed to Tenji in the *Man'yōshū*. This poem is also found in the *Gosenshū* and the *Shinkokinshū*.

2. Emperor Jitō, the forty-first emperor (645–702; r. 690?–697). She was the second daughter of Emperor Tenji and the wife of Tenmu. Jitō has two *chōka* and two *tanka* in the *Man'yōshū* and one poem in the *Shinkokinshū*.

3. Kakinomoto no Hitomaro (dates unknown; d.c. 707). He was a court poet under Emperors Jitō and Monmu. This poem is a variant of a *Man'yōshū* poem given therein as anonymous. Another variant appears in the *Shūishū* and yet another in the *Shinkokinshū*. Fully attributed to him in the *Man'yōshū* are eighteen *chōka* and seventy *tanka*. He was considered the greatest of the four great *Man'yō* poets; the others are Yamabe no Akahito, Yamanoue no Okura, and Ōtomo no Yakamochi. Only Yamanoue no Okura is omitted from the *Hyakunin Isshu*. Later scholars class Hitomaro as the first of the four greatest Japanese poets ever, followed by Teika, Sōgi, and Bashō. He was known for unconditional devotion to Jitō and the imperial family. Later, he was deified as the god of poetry. He appears in Ki no Tsurayuki's list later known as the Six Poetic Geniuses (*Rokkasen*) and in Fujiwara no Kintō's list of Thirty-Six Poetic Geniuses.

4. Yamabe no Akahito (dates unknown). He was a court poet in the early Nara period, has thirteen *chōka* and thirty-seven *tanka* in the *Man'yōshū*, and is listed by Kintō among his Thirty-Six Poetic Geniuses.

5. Sarumaru Dayū. The dates of his lifespan are unknown, but it is likely that he was active before the second half of the eighth century. He was a senior adjutant minister. This poem is in the *Kokinshū*, but listed anonymously. Listed by Kintō in his Thirty-Six Poetic Geniuses. There is a late *Sarumaru Dayūshū*, but it is of doubtful authenticity.

6. Ōtomo no Yakamochi (718–785). A Middle Counselor, he has 46 *chōka* and 430 *tanka* in the *Man'yōshū*. The final four books of the *Man'yōshū* seem like a kind of diary of Yakamochi's, giving rise to the theory that he must be the compiler of all four books. He has sixty-two poems in imperial anthologies and is one of Kintō's Thirty-Six Poetic Geniuses.

7. Abe no Nakamaro (701–770). He was sent on a mission to China, where he made friends with Li Bo and Wang Mojie. He was noticed by the Tang emperor Xuanzong, who inducted him into his entourage. At age thirty-eight he was made Director of Protections and put in control of the Three Offices (arms, arsenal, and palace guards). In 753 he was permitted to leave for home, but suffered a shipwreck and returned to Chang'an, where he remained until his death.

8. Priest Kisen. His dates are unknown, but he was likely active in the mid-ninth century. Next to nothing is known of him but what can be deduced from this one poem. He is included in Tsurayuki's Six Poetic Geniuses and mentioned by Tsurayuki in the famous Japanese Preface to the *Kokinshū*.

9. Ono no Komachi. Her lifespan dates are unknown, but she was likely active in the mid-ninth century. She was the granddaughter of Ono no Takamura (poem 11) and active in the reigns of Emperors Montoku and Seiwa. Only twenty-one poems in the *Kokinshū* and *Gosenshū* are considered authentic. A late *Komachishū* is dubious. There are many legends concerning her life, including seven extant Nō plays, five of them in the regular repertory, and a new Nō play, *Fumigara* (The Love Letters), by Tsumura Kimiko (1902–1974). She is in Kintō's Thirty-Six Poetic Geniuses and is the only woman in Tsurayuki's Six Poetic Geniuses.

10. Semimaru (dates unknown). He was likely active in the early tenth century, but nothing is known for certain about him. He is said to have lived as a hermit near the Osaka Barrier. A legend grew around him that he was a son of Emperor Daigo banished because of his blindness (seen as a retribution for sins in a past life) and a virtuoso *biwa* lutanist. He is the subject of the great Zeami Nō play, *Semimaru*. There are four poems attributed to him in imperial anthologies.

11. Ono no Takamura (802–852). A state councilor, he was a leading poet of his day, renowned for his erudition, Chinese composition, and calligraphy. In 838 he was attached to Fujiwara no Tsunetsugu's embassy to China. He feigned illness and was banished to Oki Island, but was pardoned and restored to favor after only a year. He was made state councilor with third court rank. He has six poems

in the *Kokinshū* and six more in later imperial anthologies and Japanese and Chinese verse in the *Wakan Rōeishū*.

12. Archbishop Henjō (816–890), also called Monastic Superior or Rector; lay name, Yoshimine no Munesada. He served under Emperor Nimmyō as captain of the bodyguard. He entered religion in 849 after the sudden demise of Emperor Nimmyō. The *Yamato Monogatari* recounts his loves and conversion. He is listed by Tsurayuki in his Six Poetic Geniuses and also in Kintō's Thirty-Six Poetic Geniuses. Some scholars consider him overrated. Others are careful to emphasize that this poem was written before he entered religion. There is a *Henjōshū* of his poems.

13. Retired Emperor Yōzei, the fifty-seventh emperor (868–949; r. 876–884). He showed signs of mental instability and was forced by his maternal uncle and regent to abdicate in favor of Kōkō. For the next sixty years, he diligently practiced poetry and presided over many poetic contests. This is his only poem in the imperial anthologies.

14. Minamoto no Tōru (822–895). He was the son of Emperor Saga and a great aesthete. Named Kawara Minister of the Left from his residence east of the Sixth Avenue near the river beach, or *kawara*, he was considered by many to have been one of the models for Genji in *The Tale of Genji*. He has two poems in both the *Kokinshū* and *Gosenshū* and is featured in Zeami's Nō, *Tōru*, and the Nō *Nishikigi*, which cites this poem.

15. Emperor Kōkō, the fifty-eighth emperor (830–887; r. 884–887). He was the third son of Emperor Ninmyō and a protégé of regent Fujiwara no Mototsune. Enthroned at age fifty-five in succession to the mentally unstable Yōzei (poem 13), he was called the Emperor of the Ninna Era. He has fourteen poems in imperial anthologies and a collection, the *Ninna Gyoshū*.

16. Ariwara no Yukihira (818–893). A middle counselor, he was the grandson of Emperor Heizei and older half-brother of Narihira (poem 17). He was governor of Inaba. There is an undocumented tradition that he was banished to Suma for three years and may have been one of the models for Genji in *The Tale of Genji*. He is mentioned

in the Chinese preface to the *Kokinshū* for skill in Chinese verse composition and has eleven poems in imperial anthologies, only eight of which are now considered authentic—four in the *Kokinshū* and four in other anthologies.

17. Ariwara no Narihira (825–880). He was the grandson of two emperors, Heizei, on his father's side, and Kanmu, on his mother's. He was long considered the hero and even the author of the *Ise Monogatari*, but this is no longer accepted by scholars. His eighty-seven poems in imperial anthologies are enough to clearly establish his reputation as one of the best poets of his time. He is listed as one of Tsurayuki's Six Poetic Geniuses and again in Kintō's Thirty-Six Poetic Geniuses.

18. Fujiwara no Toshiyuki (d. 901). He was a celebrated calligrapher who served under four emperors. In 897 he became captain of the guard of the right. He has twenty-eight poems in imperial anthologies and a private collection, the *Toshiyukishū*. He is one of Kintō's Thirty-Six Poetic Geniuses.

19. Lady Ise (also known as Ise no Go; c. 875–c. 938). She was a lady-in-waiting and favorite of Emperor Uda, then of his son Atsuyoshi with whom she had a child. She has 22 poems in the *Kokinshū*, 72 in the *Gosenshū*, and 184 poems in the combined imperial anthologies.

20. Prince Motoyoshi (890–943). He was the eldest son of Emperor Yōzei and figures in several tales of the *Yamato Monogatari*. He was famous as a lover. Twenty of his poems are in the imperial anthologies.

21. Priest Sosei (dates unknown); lay name, Yoshimine no Harutoshi. The son of Yoshimine no Munesada, Archbishop Henjō (cf. poem 12), he is said to have entered religion at the urging of his father. A renowned calligrapher, he has thirty-six poems in the *Kokinshū* and as many as sixty-two in the combined imperial anthologies, as well as being one of Kintō's Thirty-Six Poetic Geniuses. A *Sosei Hōshishū* exists.

22. Fun'ya (also known as Bun'ya) no Yasuhide. His lifespan dates are unknown, but he probably lived in the second half of the ninth century. He was a provincial official who was appointed second

director of the wardrobe in 879, perhaps in recognition of his poetic talent rather than any specific administrative competence. Mentioned in both the Chinese and Japanese prefaces to the *Kokinshū*, he has six poems in the imperial anthologies, five of them in the *Kokinshū*. He is listed among Tsurayuki's Six Poetic Geniuses, though some scholars believe that Tsurayuki overrated him.

23. Ōe no Chisato (fl. c. 889–923). He was the nephew of Yukihira (poem 16) and Narihira (poem 17) and a low-ranking officer of the guard. For unknown reasons, he was banished to the province of Iyo (present-day Ehime prefecture). He is known for his collection *Kudai Waka* (110 poems, each based on a line of Chinese poetry), dedicated in 894 to Emperor Uda, who had also ordered them. Twenty-five of his poems appear in the imperial anthologies.

24. Sugawara no Michizane (845–903). He is sometimes referred to as Kanke, which means "Sugawara Family," the third generation of the Sugawara family to use that pseudonym. Appointed minister of the right, he showed complete loyalty to Emperors Uda and Daigo. He fell afoul of Fujiwara no Tokihira, as depicted in the Kabuki play *Shihei no Nanawarai*. He was named governor of Dazaifu, where he went in virtual exile and died there about a year later. Calamities of every kind followed his death. Efforts were made to placate his supposedly angry spirit, mainly by deifying him as Kitano Tenjin. He was later dubbed Tenjin God of Letters and is to this day earnestly prayed to by students before exams. This poem was cited by the great fifteenth-century *renga* master, Priest Sōgi, in his *Tsukushi no Michi no Ki*, a travel diary of a pilgrimage to Dazaifu. Michizane left a considerable body of work in Chinese and Japanese and a new *Man'yōshū*, the *Shinsen Man'yōshū*. Cf. Zeami Nō, *Oimatsu*.

25. Fujiwara no Sadakata (873–932). The father of Asatada (poem 44), he was third ward minister of the right. He has eighteen poems in the imperial anthologies, one in the *Kokinshū* and a *kashū*.

26. Fujiwara no Tadahira (posthumous name Teishinkō; 880–949). The grand chancellor and grand minister, he was the younger brother of Tokihira, whom he succeeded as head of the clan. He has

seven poems in the *Gosenshū* and six more in later imperial anthologies, as well as a diary, called the *Teishinkōki*.
27. Fujiwara no Kanesuke (877–933), called Tsutsumi Chunagon, middle counselor of the embankment, because his residence was near the dam on the Kamogawa river. A cousin of Sadakata (poem 25), he had a long association with the compilers of the *Kokinshū*, Ki no Tsurayuki (poem 35), Ōshikōchi no Mitsune (poem 29), and others. He has fifty-seven poems in the imperial anthologies, a private *kashū*. He is one of Kintō's Thirty-Six Poetic Geniuses.
28. Lord Minamoto no Muneyuki (d. 939). He was the grandson of Emperor Kōkō (poem 15) and has fifteen poems in the imperial anthologies, six of them in the *Kokinshū*, and a *kashū*. He is one of Kintō's Thirty-Six Poetic Geniuses.
29. Ōshikōchi no Mitsune. His lifespan dates are unknown, but he appears to have died c. 925. He had a modest career, but is one of the compilers of the *Kokinshū*, and, with Tsurayuki, the best represented poet in that collection. He has 196 poems in imperial anthologies after the *Kokinshū* and a large number of *byōbu-uta* (poems on screens), many cited in records of *uta-awase* poem contests. He is one of Kintō's Thirty-Six Poetic Geniuses.
30. Mibu no Tadamine (dates uncertain). His birth date is sometimes given as c. 850. He was the father of Tadami (poem 41). He helped edit the *Kokinshū* and left a *kashū*, *Tadamineshū*, and a treatise on poetry. He has eighty-two poems in the imperial anthologies, thirty-five of them in the *Kokinshū*.
31. Sakanoue no Korenori (dates unknown). He had a modest career as a minor official, ending as governor of Kaga. He won his greatest glory as a *kemari* football champion. He left a private *kashū* and forty-one poems in the imperial anthologies, of which eight are in the *Kokinshū*. He is one of Kintō's Thirty-Six Poetic Geniuses.
32. Harumichi no Tsuraki (d. 920). He died shortly after being appointed governor of Oki, before he could reach his post. He has three poems in the *Kokinshū* and two in the *Gosenshū*.
33. Ki no Tomonori (d. 905 or 906, exact dates unknown). A cousin of Tsurayuki (poem 35), he helped with the compilation of the *Kokinshū*,

but died shortly after its completion (elegy in his memory in Bk. XVI, 838). He has forty-six poems in the *Kokinshū* and over twenty more in later imperial anthologies. He is among Kintō's Thirty-Six Poetic Geniuses.

34. Fujiwara no Okikaze (dates unknown). He participated in numerous poetry competitions and was a reputed koto musician. He published seventeen poems in the *Kokinshū* and twenty-one in later imperial anthologies. He left a *kashū*. He was one of Kintō's Thirty-Six Poetic Geniuses.

35. Ki no Tsurayuki (868–945). He was the chief compiler of the *Kokinshū* and wrote its famous Japanese preface. He led the battle to have Japanese poetry seen as the equal of Chinese verse. He has 202 poems in the *Kokinshū* (comprising nearly 10 percent). In 930 he was appointed governor of Tosa in Shikoku. In the persona of a woman, he wrote a famous diary, the *Tosa Nikki*, about his journey from Tosa back to Kyoto. He was considered the greatest poet of his time. He had 452 works in imperial anthologies, 102 of them in the *Kokinshū*. He also has a big *kashū*. He is listed as one of Kintō's Thirty-Six Poetic Geniuses.

36. Kiyohara no Fukayabu (dates unknown). He was a descendant of Prince Toneri, the founder of Nara, ancestor of Motosuke (poem 42), and great-grandfather of Sei Shōnagon (poem 62). He published forty-one poems in imperial anthologies, of which seventeen are in the *Kokinshū* and also wrote a *kashū*.

37. Fun'ya no Asayasu (a.k.a Tomoyasu; dates unknown). The son of Yasuhide (poem 22), he was a low-ranking official. He participated in many poetry competitions. Three of his poems appear in the imperial anthologies.

38. Ukon (dates unknown). The daughter or younger sister of Suenawa, captain of the left bodyguards, called the Katano captain, a notoriously amorous man, she also had pronounced amorous proclivities. *Yamato Monogatari* [Tales of Yamato] gives several accounts of her love affairs with Fujiwara nobles and others. She was a lady-in-waiting to Empress Onshi, Emperor Daigo's consort. Nine of her poems appear in the imperial anthologies.

39. Minamoto no Hitoshi (880–951). A state councilor, he was the

great-grandson of Emperor Saga. After serving as governor in important provinces, in 947 he was appointed Sangi Counselor with Fourth Court Rank. Four of his poems appear in the *Gosenshū*.

40. Taira no Kanemori (d. 990). A descendant of Emperor Kōkō (poem 46), he ended his career as governor of Suruga. Eighty-seven of his poems appeared in imperial anthologies, and three poems listed as "anonymous" in the *Gosenshū* are considered his. He also wrote a *kashū* and was one of Kintō's Thirty-Six Poetic Geniuses.

41. Mibu no Tadami (dates unknown). The son of Tadamine (poem 30), he was appointed grand comptroller of the province of Settsu but nothing else is known of his career. Thirty-seven of his poems appear in imperial anthologies, and he left a *kashū*. He is listed as one of Kintō's Thirty-Six Poetic Geniuses.

42. Kiyohara no Motosuke (908–990). The grandson of Fukayabu (poem 36), he was the father of Sei Shōnagon (poem 62) and governor of Higo, present-day Kumamoto. He was attached to the Bureau of Poetry in 951 and assisted in the compilation of the *Gosenshū* and transcription of the *Man'yōshū*. He participated in most poetry competitions of his day. 106 of his poems appear in imperial anthologies. He is one of Kintō's Thirty-Six Poetic Geniuses.

43. Fujiwara no Atsutada (906–943). The third son of Tokihira, he was a renowned musician and very handsome. There are tales of his amorous escapades in many books, including the *Yamato Monogatari*. Thirty of his poems appear in imperial anthologies, and he also has a *kashū*. He is one of Kintō's Thirty-Six Poetic Geniuses.

44. Fujiwara no Asatada (a.k.a Tomotada; 910–966). He was a middle counselor. The fifth son of Sadakata (poem 25), he has twenty-one poems in imperial anthologies and is one of Kintō's Thirty-Six Poetic Geniuses.

45. Lord Kentoku, Fujiwara no Koremasa (also read Koretada; 924–972). Regent and Grand Minister, he was named Ichijō (of the First Ward). In 951, he was appointed Director of the Bureau of Poetry. The *Gosenshū* was compiled under his direction. He has a *kashū* (The Collected Poems of the First Ward Regent) and thirty-seven poems in imperial anthologies.

46. Sone no Yoshitada (dates unknown). He flourished in the second

half of the tenth century. Not much is known of him except that he was a *jō* (secretary) in Tango, hence his sobriquets Sotango and Sotan. Seen as an eccentric, he was not much valued in his lifetime. However, in the twelfth century, he was hailed as an innovator, which explains why eighty-nine of his poems appear in imperial anthologies. There is a *Yoshitada Hyakushu* (a hundred-poem sequence).

47. Priest Egyō (sometimes read Ekei; dates unknown, but probably second half of the tenth century). He was counted in another famous list of poets, the *Chūko Sanjūrokkasen* (Late Classical Thirty-Six Poetic Geniuses). Fifty-six of his poems appear in *Shūishū* and later imperial anthologies. He also left a *kashū*.

48. Minamoto no Shigeyuki (d. c. 1000). The great-grandson of Emperor Seiwa and governor of Sagami (present-day Kanagawa), he accompanied Fujiwara no Sanekata (poem 51) when he took up his post as governor of Mutsu (present-day Aomori), where both died. Sixty-seven of his poems appear in the *Shūishū* and later imperial anthologies. He left a *kashū* and is listed among Kintō's Thirty-Six Poetic Geniuses.

49. Ōnakatomi no Yoshinobu (921–991). Scholars see the possibility here of a false attribution. He was Hereditary High Official of the Department of Religious Affairs (Shinto) and, beginning in 951, a member of the Bureau of Poetry. He participated in the transcription of the *Man'yōshū* and compilation of the *Gosenshū*. He published 125 poems in imperial anthologies and wrote a *kashū*. He was one of Kintō's Thirty-Six Poetic Geniuses.

50. Fujiwara no Yoshitaka (954–974). The son of Koretada (poem 45), he was captain of the right bodyguards. He died of smallpox at age twenty on the same day as his twin brother. He was the father of the renowned calligrapher Yukinari. Twelve of his poems appear in imperial anthologies. He left a *kashū* and was one of the Late Classical Thirty-Six Poetic Geniuses.

51. Fujiwara no Sanekata (d. 994). He was the great-grandson of Teishinkō (poem 26) and commander of the bodyguard. In 995, he was appointed governor of Mutsu (present-day Aomori) where he

remained until his death. He was cited as a lover of Sei Shōnagon. Sixty-seven of his poems appear in imperial anthologies, and he left a *kashū*.

52. Fujiwara no Michinobu (972–994). A son of Tamemitsu, he was adopted by Kaneie. Although he died at twenty-three he was considered a brilliant albeit short-lived commander of the guard. Forty-eight of his poems appear in imperial anthologies. He wrote a *kashū*, and was one of the Late Classical Thirty-Six Poetic Geniuses.

53. Mother of Michitsuna (c. 937–995). A Fujiwara lady noted for exceptional beauty, she was the secondary consort of Kaneie (grand minister and regent). She was the author of the *Kagerō Nikki*. Thirty-six of her poems appear in imperial anthologies, and she wrote a *kashū*. She was one of the Late Classical Thirty-Six Poetic Geniuses.

54. Takako, mother of the Honorary Grand Minister (d. 996). The wife of the Grand Chancellor Michitaka, she had several children, among them Empress Teishi (Sei Shōnagon's empress) and Korechika, who, after being minister of the right, was forced out of office by his uncle Michinaga and given the grandiloquent but empty new title of honorary grand minister.

55. Fujiwara no Kintō (966–1041). He was the son of the Grand Minister Yoritada. He was a grand counselor but after his daughter died, he entered religion and retired to a valley in the hills to the north of Kyoto. His home became a meeting place for the best poets and minds of his day, who all deferred to his judgment in matters poetic. He edited the *Wakan Rōeishū* (c. 1013), wrote treatises on the art of poetry, and organized poetry competitions. He drew up the most famous of the many lists of Thirty-Six Poetic Geniuses and left a considerable body of critical writings and poetry in Chinese and Japanese. Eighty-nine of his poems appeared in imperial anthologies. He left a *kashū*.

56. Izumi Shikibu (b. c. 976–c. 978). She was the daughter of Ōe no Masamune, governor of Echizen (present-day Fukui) and wife of Tachibana no Michisada, governor of Izumi (present-day Osaka fu). Her daughter was KoShikibu (poem 60). The lover of Prince

Tametaka and then Prince Atsumichi, she was lady-in-waiting along with Murasaki Shikibu (poem 57) of Empress Shōshi. Izumi Shikibu is considered by many to have been the greatest woman poet of the Heian period, a time when supremely talented women flourished. She has 242 poems in imperial anthologies and two *kashū*. She was one of the Late Classical Thirty-Six Poetic Geniuses.

57. Murasaki Shikibu (c. 978–c. 1014). She was a lady-in-waiting to Empress Shōshi and a prolific poet, giving some 800 *waka* as attributions to the characters in her great work *The Tale of Genji*. She always apologizes for the poor quality of these *waka*, but many connoisseurs find great merit in them. She left a diary and a *kashū*. She has sixty poems in imperial anthologies and was one of the Late Classical Thirty-Six Poetic Geniuses.

58. Daini no Sanmi (Fujiwara no Katako; b. c. 999). She was the daughter of Murasaki Shikibu (poem 57) and Fujiwara no Nobutaka and the nurse of Emperor GoReizei. Some attribute to her the final ten chapters of *The Tale of Genji*. Thirty-seven of her poems appear in imperial anthologies. She left a *kashū*.

59. Akazome Emon (dates unknown). She is said to have been over eighty in 1041 and was lady-in-waiting to Empress Shōshi at the same time as Izumi and Murasaki. Murasaki in her diary gives a very unflattering account of Emon under her married name of Masahira Emon (her husband was Ōe no Masahira). She was the author or coauthor of *Eiga Monogatari*. Ninety-three of her poems appear in imperial anthologies. She left a *kashū* and was one of the Late Classical Thirty-Six Poetic Geniuses.

60. KoShikibu (d. 1025). She was the daughter of Tachibana no Michisada and Izumi Shikibu (poem 56) and, like her mother, lady-in-waiting to Empress Shōshi. She had a son with the grand chancellor, Norimichi. She died before she was thirty and left just four poems in imperial anthologies.

61. Ise no Taifu (not to be confused with the Lady Ise, poem 19; dates unknown). She was the granddaughter of Ōnakatomi no Yoshinobu (poem 49) and lady-in-waiting to Empress Shōshi. Fifty-one of her poems appear in imperial anthologies. She left a *kashū* and was one of the Late Classical Thirty-Six Poetic Geniuses.

62. Sei Shōnagon (c. 965–c. 1025). She was the daughter of Kiyohara no Motosuke (poem 42), great-granddaughter of Kiyohara no Fukayabu (poem 36), and lady-in-waiting to Empress Teishi. She wrote *Makura no Sōshi*, the famous *Pillow Book*. With Murasaki Shikibu and Izumi Shikibu, she is considered one of the greatest of the outstanding women writers of the Heian period. She has fourteen poems in imperial anthologies and left a *kashū*. Formerly she was cited as a possible model for the legend of Komachi. She was one of the Late Classical Thirty-Six Poetic Geniuses.

63. Fujiwara no Michimasa (992–1054). The son of Minister Korechika, he was removed from power as master of West Kyoto by Michinaga. He had an affair with Princess Tōshi, former High-Priestess of Ise Grand Shrine, which earned him the ire of Emperor Sanjō in 1016 and after that led the life of a dilettante recluse. Six of his poems appear in imperial anthologies.

64. Fujiwara no Sadayori (995–1045). A supernumerary middle counselor, he was the eldest son of Kintō (poem 55). On his mother's side, he was a grandson of Emperor Murakami. He served as director for military affairs and after that as middle counselor. Koshikibu's poem (60) was dedicated to him. He was renowned as a poet and calligrapher. He has forty-five poems in imperial anthologies and left a *kashū*. He is listed among the Late Classical Thirty-Six Poetic Geniuses.

65. Sagami (b. c. 1000). She was said to be a daughter of Minamoto no Yorimitsu (a.k.a. Raikō), who appears in the Nō play *Tsuchi Gumo*. Her husband, Ōe no Kin'yori, had been governor of Sagami (present-day Kanagawa). She participated in many poetry competitions. She published 109 poems in imperial anthologies and left a *kashū*. She is listed as one of the Late Classical Thirty-Six Poetic Geniuses.

66. Prelate Gyōson (1055–1135). The son of Minamoto no Motohira, he entered Onjōji Temple (a.k.a. Miidera in Ōtsu, where Ernest Fenollosa's ashes are partially interred). He practiced the Shugendō austerities of the *yamabushi* mountain ascetics for many years, before becoming Superior General of Enryakuji, the highest prelate of the Tendai sect, in 1123 and Grand Almoner of Emperor Shirakawa and

Emperor Toba. He published forty-eight poems in imperial anthologies and left a *kashū*.

67. Court Handmaid Suō, Nakako (dates unknown). Daughter of Taira no Munenaka, governor of Suō, she was handmaiden in the inner service (*naishi*) of four emperors, from Emperor GoReizei to Emperor Horikawa. She entered religion in 1108 and died shortly afterward. Thirty-five of her poems appeared in imperial anthologies. She left a *kashū*.

68. Retired Emperor Sanjō (976–1017; r. 1011–1016), sixty-seventh emperor. The son of Emperor Reizei, he became crown prince in 986. He was a grandson through his mother of Fujiwara no Kaneie. Eight of his poems appeared in imperial anthologies.

69. Priest Nōin (988–1051); lay name, Tachibana no Nagayasu. He was a student of Chinese literature and entered religion at age twenty-six. He began his religious life as a peregrinating poet and ascetic and finally settled in Settsu at Kosobe. He is the author of a famous treatise on poetry, *Nōin Utamakura*. Sixty-five of his poems appeared in imperial anthologies. He left a *kashū* and is listed among the Late Classical Thirty-Six Poetic Geniuses.

70. Priest Ryōzen (dates unknown, but fl. around 998–1064). A Tendai monk and then abbot of Gion monastery, he lived as a hermit at Ōhara and, at the end of his life, in Unrin'in. Thirty-one of his poems appeared in imperial anthologies.

71. Minamoto no Tsunenobu (1016–1097). A major counselor, he was renowned as a poet and musician. At the age of nearly eighty he was appointed governor of Dazaifu, at that time tantamount to banishment. He died there two years later. He published eighty-six poems in imperial anthologies and left a *kashū*. He is counted as one of the Late Classical Thirty-Six Poetic Geniuses.

72. Lady Kii (dates unknown). She was a lady-in-waiting to Empress Genshi, consort of Emperor GoSuzaku, then lady-in-waiting to his eldest daughter, Princess Yūshi. Thirty-one of her poems appear in imperial anthologies. She left a *kashū* called *Ichi no Miya no Kii Shū*.

73. Ōe no Masafusa (1041–1111). A GonChūnagon (supernumerary middle counselor) from a famous lettered family, he was a child prodigy

in Chinese studies. He was the favorite and confidant of retired Emperor Horikawa and a brilliant administrator. Following in the footsteps of his revered Sugawara no Michizane, he served as governor of Dazaifu. He rose to become director of the Treasury, but died soon after this appointment. He left an important body of work in Chinese and Japanese. He published 119 poems in imperial anthologies and left a *kashū*, the *Gō no Sochishū*.

74. Minamoto no Toshiyori (1055–1129). The son of Tsunenobu (poem 71), he was considered the best poet in the entourage of that renowned connoisseur of poetry Emperor Horikawa (1079–1107). He was the compiler of the *Kin'yōshū* and the author of a famous poetry treatise, the *Toshiyori Zuinō*. He had 209 poems in imperial anthologies and wrote a *kashū*. He engaged in a famous polemic with Fujiwara no Mototoshi about "the new mode" of writing poetry.

75. Fujiwara no Mototoshi (1060–1142). The son of Minister Toshiie, he had only reached the rank of Lieutenant of the Gate Guards when he entered religion in 1138 at the age of nearly eighty, taking the name Kakushin. He was a highly respected poet, chief of the "old style," as opposed to Toshiyori, who advocated the "new style." His failure to gain promotion may have had something to do with his being considered old-fashioned by his contemporaries. He was the judge of many poetry contests. He had 105 poems in imperial anthologies and left a *kashū*. He was one of the Late Classical Thirty-Six Poetic Geniuses.

76. Fujiwara no Tadamichi (1097–1164). A former prime minister and chancellor, he was the Hosshōji Buddhist Novice. He was the son of Grand Chancellor Tadazane, father of Jien (poem 95) and elder brother of Yorinaga, who was known as "Yorinaga the Bad," and he is one of the principal characters in the *Hōgen Monogatari* (1156). Poem 75 is addressed to him. He was reputed highly as a poet in both Chinese and Japanese and had fifty-eight poems in imperial anthologies. He also left a *kashū* as well as a collection of Chinese verse.

77. Retired Emperor Sutoku (1119–1164; r. 1123–1141), seventy-fifth emperor. He succeeded his father, Emperor Toba, but he was forced to

abdicate in favor of his brother, Konoe. When Konoe died at age seventeen, Sutoku fomented the Hōgen Rebellion (1156) with former Minister of the Left, Yorinaga the Bad. He was vanquished and then exiled to Sanuki in Shikoku. A respected poet himself, he ordered the compilation of the *Shikashū* by Akisuke (poem 79). He had seventy-eight poems in imperial anthologies.

78. Minamoto no Kanemasa (dates unknown, but fl. at the end of the eleventh to the beginning of twelfth century). He was one of a group in retired Emperor Horikawa's circle. He published seven poems in imperial anthologies.

79. Fujiwara no Akisuke (1090–1155). The master of West Kyoto, he was the father of Kiyosuke (poem 84) and received an order in 1144 from Emperor Sutoku to compile the *Shikashū*, which he completed in 1151. He had eighty-four poems in imperial anthologies and left a *kashū*.

80. Horikawa (dates unknown). She was a lady-in-waiting to the daughter of Emperor Horikawa, who became the Princess Priestess of the Grand Shrine of Ise. Then she became a lady-in-waiting to Taikenmon In, the consort of Emperor Toba. In 1143 she entered religion, along with her mistress. Sixty-six of her poems appeared in imperial anthologies, and she left a *kashū*. She was one of the Late Classical Thirty-Six Poetic Geniuses.

81. Fujiwara no Sanesada (1139–1191). He was the nephew of Toshinari (poem 93) and a cousin of Teika (poem 97). He was removed from his post as Tokudaiji Minister of the Left under the Heike regime, but after their defeat in the naval battle of Dan-no-Ura in 1185, he was made the minister of the left in 1189 (see *The Tale of Heike*). Two years later, already ill, he entered religion and then died not long afterward. He was renowned as a musician as well as a poet. He left a diary, a *kashū*, and seventy-eight poems in imperial anthologies.

82. Priest Dōin (1090–c. 1179). The Lieutenant of the Stables of the Left, he entered religion in 1172. His private poetry collections have not survived, but forty-one of his poems appear in imperial anthologies.

83. Fujiwara no Shunzei or Toshinari (1114–1204). The master of the empress dowager's palace, he was the great poetic arbiter of his time

and the father of Teika, the editor of the *Hyakunin Isshu*. He entered religion in 1176. A protégé of Emperor Toba, he adopted the "new style" of Minamoto no Toshiyori (poem 74). He was a judge of many poetry competitions, and about 2,000 of his judgments on poetry contests (*uta-awase*) have survived. He compiled the *Senzaishū* and authored several theoretic treatises on poetry, a *kashū*, and some 418 poems in imperial anthologies. Associated with him are the very important aesthetic concepts of *sabi* (loneliness), *yōen* (ethereal beauty), and *yūgen* (mystery and depth). The last of these concepts has great importance in Nō drama (see the Nō plays *Tadanori* by Zeami and *Shunzei Tadanori* by Naitō Tozaemon). The Irish poet W.B. Yeats was attracted by the concept of *yūgen*, and it influenced his own Nō plays. *Sabi* was a major ideal of the *renga* poets and of the haiku derived from *renga*'s *hokku*. Famous examples of this may be found in the haiku of Bashō.

84. Fujiwara no Kiyosuke (1104–1177). The second son of Akisuke (poem 79), he was adjutant majordomo of the empress dowager. He was in frequent conflict with his father, but eventually inherited the headship of the famous Rokujō school of poetry from him. He received an order from Emperor Nijō to compile a sequel to the *Shikashū*, but because this emperor died before its completion, this *Shoku Shikashū* was not officially classified as an imperial anthology. He was the author of two of the most famous poetic treatises, *Ōgishō* (The Book of Arcana) and *Fukurozōshi*. He left a *kashū* and ninety-four poems in imperial anthologies, and was one of the Late Classical Poetic Geniuses.

85. Priest Shun'e (1113–c. 1191). The son of Minamoto no Toshiyori (poem 74), he was the mentor of Kamo no Chōmei (1153–1216), who wrote the *Hōjōki*. Kamo no Chōmei recorded in his *Mumyōshō* many of the master's words. Shun'e authored theoretical writings and made several compilations. He left a *kashū* and eighty-three poems in imperial anthologies and was one of the Late Classical Thirty-Six Poetic Geniuses.

86. Priest Saigyō (1118–1190); lay name, Satō Norikiyo. An Officer of the Left Guard, he was a friend of Shunzei (poem 83). He abandoned

his wife and family and entered religion at the age of twenty-three. Famous as a peregrinating poet monk, he was considered the greatest poet of Japan by his emulator, the haiku master Bashō. He was poet of the moon and cherry blossoms and solitude and compiled several private collections of poetry, the most famous being the *Sankashū* (Mountain Anthology), in which poem 86 can be found. A total of 248 of his poems appear in imperial anthologies. Concerning Saigyō, the moon and love and so on, see Zeami's *Eguchi*.

87. Priest Jakuren (1139–1202); lay name, Fujiwara no Sadanaga. A nephew and adopted son of Toshinari (poem 83), he belonged to the Mikohidari house with Teika (poem 97) and Ietaka (poem 98). He entered religion in 1192, was appointed a member of the Bureau of Poetry in 1201, and participated in the compilation of *Shinkokinshū*, but died before it was completed. He left a *kashū* and 117 poems in imperial anthologies.

88. Kōkamon In no Bettō (dates unknown). The daughter of Minamoto no Toshitaka, she was lady-in-waiting to Empress Seishi, later known as Kōkamon In. She has only nine poems in imperial anthologies.

89. Princess Shokushi (a.k.a Shikishi; d. 1201). Daughter of Emperor GoShirakawa. She served as the Kamo Priestess 1159–1169. She studied poetry under Shunzei and later under Teika. Tradition has it that it was for her that Shunzei wrote his treatise *Korai Fūteishō* (Some Notes on the Old Style). Although she was much older, there is a tradition that she and Teika were lovers. However, this is unlikely. Cf. Zeami's play *Teika*. A *kashū* and 155 poems in imperial anthologies.

90. Inpumon In no Taifu (dates unknown, but she is said to have been about seventy in 1200). The daughter of Fujiwara no Nobunari, she served as a lady in waiting to a daughter of Emperor GoShirakawa, Princess Ryōshi (Inpumon In), and took part in many poetry contests. She was highly esteemed by Teika and left a *kashū* and sixty-three poems in imperial anthologies.

91. Fujiwara no Yoshitsune (1169–1206). The son of Grand Chancellor Kanezane, he was the nephew of Jien (poem 95). He served as minis-

ter of the Left in 1199, Gokyōgoku Regent in 1200, and grand minister in 1204. He was also a member of the Bureau of Poetry and took part in the compilation of the *Shinkokinshū*, for which he wrote the preface. He left a *kashū* and 319 poems in imperial anthologies and was one of the Late Classical Thirty-Six Poetic Geniuses.

92. Lady Sanuki (c. 1141–1217). The daughter of Minamoto no Yorimasa, one of the main characters of the story of a conflict of 1159 the *Heiji Monogatari* (The Tale of Heiji) and *The Tale of Heike*, as well as Zeami's Nō *Yorimasa*. She was lady-in-waiting to GoToba's empress, Ninshi. Seventy-three of her poems appear in imperial anthologies. She was one of the Late Classical Thirty-Six Poetic Geniuses.

93. Minamoto no Sanetomo (1192–1219). The third Kamakura shogun, he studied poetry from childhood and was taught by Teika. Teika, who was anything but a flatterer, praised Sanetomo as having surpassed himself at the early age of twenty. Teika's *Kindai Shūka* (Superior Poems of Our Times) is said to have been written as a manual for Sanetomo's instruction. The compilation of these kinds of instruction manuals for students of poetry was common at the time, as the students were expected to be completely familiar with great "classic" poems before composing themselves. Sometimes they would incorporate elements of the these originals in their own efforts. Sanetomo was a virtual prisoner of his family on his mother's side. He had a drinking problem and was encouraged to drink tea, which seems to have been the start of the close connection between the warrior class and that beverage. Considered, with Saigyō, as the greatest poets of their day, he was nevertheless assassinated at the age of twenty-eight. He left a *kashū*, *Kinkaishū* (Collection of Flakes of Gold), as well as ninety-three poems in imperial anthologies.

94. Fujiwara no Masatsune (1170–1221). A state councilor, he founded the Asukai school of *Kemari* (Japanese football). In 1198 GoToba summoned him from Kamakura and in 1201 assigned him to the Bureau of Poetry. He took part in the compilation of the *Shinkokinshū*. He left a *kashū* and 134 poems in imperial anthologies and was one of the Late Classical Thirty-Six Poetic Geniuses.

95. Ex High Prelate Jien (1155–1225). The son of a grand counselor,

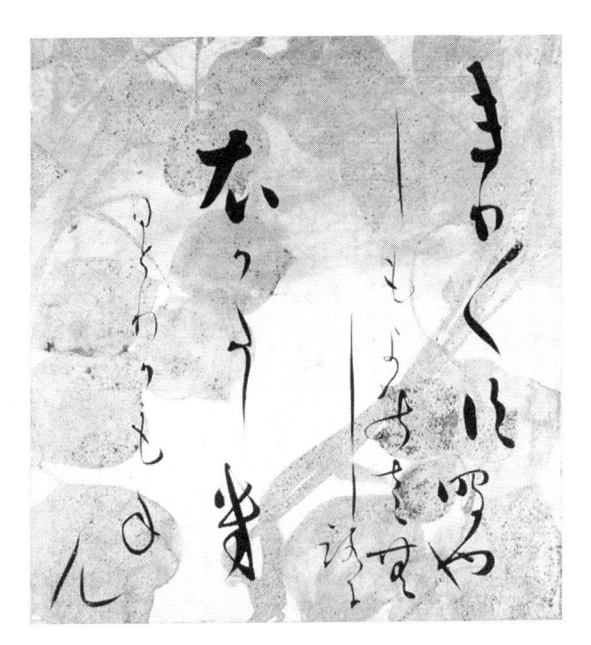

Figure 6. Kudzu-zu. *Poem* (Shin Kokin Wakashū, *no. 518*) *(91 in the* Hyakunin Isshu *but with slight variations in the text). Square paper* (shikishi) *with ground painting of kudzu vine. Calligraphy by Hon'ami Kōetsu. Painting attributed to Tawaraya Sōtatsu. From the* Shikishijō, *an album of poems from the* Shin Kokin Wakashū. *Calligraphy by Hon'ami Kōetsu (d. c. 1640). 36 leaves in total. Ink and color on paper, Edo period (seventeenth century). (Gotoh Museum)*

Fujiwara no Tadamichi (poem 76) was a brother of Kanezane and uncle of Yoshitsune (poem 91). He entered religion in 1165 and became superior general of Tendai in 1192, after having served as grand almoner to Emperor GoToba since 1184. He was a poet in the circle of Toshinari (poem 83) and of his nephew Yoshitsune (poem 86). He is most famous for his *Gukanshō* (A Modest Look at History), an important work in which he seeks to find the meaning of history from a Buddhist perspective. He was also a member of the

Bureau of Poetry. He left a *kashū* and some 267 poems in imperial anthologies and was one of the Late Classical Thirty-Six Poetic Geniuses.

96. Fujiwara no Kintsune (1171–1244). A former chancellor and a lay novice, he served as grand minister in 1222. He entered religion in 1231. He founded the illustrious Sai'onji subclan of the Fujiwara clan. His elder sister was Teika's wife. He was one of the best poets of his time and had 114 poems included in imperial anthologies.

97. Fujiwara no Teika (Sadaie; 1162–1241). The son of Toshinari (poem 83), he was a supernumerary middle counselor. He helped compile the *Shinkokinshū* (1206) and was sole editor of *Shin Chokusenshū* (1236), for which he also wrote the preface. A philologist, he conserved many important Heian writings, e.g., *The Tale of Genji* and authored several treatises and collections. He wrote a diary, called the *Meigetsuki*. He is said to have been physically unattractive and irascible, but was recognized as a great poet as well as authority on and judge of poetry. The compiler of the *Ogura Hyakunin Isshu*, he published 465 poems in imperial anthologies and left a *kashū*, *Shūigūsō*.

98. Fujiwara no Ietaka (Karyū; 1158–1237). The director of Palace Affairs, he was one of the compilers of *Shinkokinshū*. He was a son-in-law of Jakuren (poem 87). He studied under Toshinari (poem 83) and was an intimate of Emperor GoToba, with whom he continued to correspond even after GoToba's banishment. He left a *kashū* and 282 poems in imperial anthologies.

99. GoToba In (1180–1239; r. 1183–1198). He was the eighty-second emperor and a son of Emperor Takakura. He was also the younger brother of Emperor Antoku, whom he succeeded at age four, after the Heike took Antoku to the western provinces. He abdicated in 1198 but remained *de facto* sovereign in the names of his sons Tsuchimikado and Juntoku. In 1221, he moved against the Kamakura shogunate, but the revolt failed. He was exiled to Oki island, where he spent the last eighteen years of his life. He was deeply interested in poetry and took part in the compilation of the *Shinkokinshū*. He also started a vogue for *renga*. He has 256 poems in imperial anthologies and left a *kashū* and a treatise on poetry (The Oral Tradition of

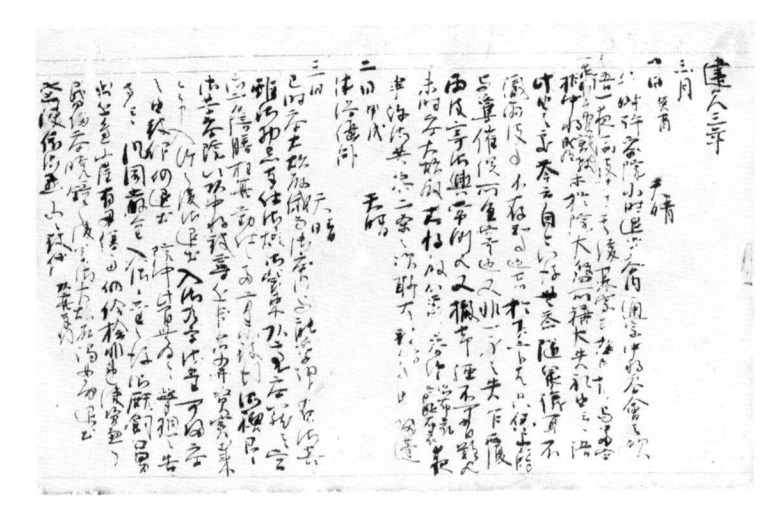

Figure 7. A Segment of Teika's Meigetsuki. *(Shiguretei, Reizei Family Archive)*

GoToba). Teika and he shared a great mutual respect, despite their frequent clashes.

100. Juntoku In (1197–1242; r. 1210–1221). He was the eighty-fourth emperor and third son of GoToba. He took part in his father's failed rebellion in 1221 and was deposed and exiled to Sado island, where he died twenty-one years later. He studied under Teika and left a large corpus of writings, notably the *Yakumo Mishō* (August Notes on the Eight Clouds), which though mostly devoted to *waka* was also one of the first treatises to deal seriously with *renga*. He left a *kashū* and 159 *waka* in imperial anthologies.

Figure 8. Hyakunin Isshu *playing cards. (Collection of Hideji Ōyagi)*

WAKA *AND ROMANIZED TRANSLITERATION OF* WAKA

1. 　　天智天皇　　　　　　　Tenji Tennō

　　　秋の田の　　　　　　　Aki no ta no
　　　かりほの庵の　　　　　kari-ho no io no
　　　苫をあらみ　　　　　　toma wo arami
　　　わが衣手は　　　　　　wa ga koromo-de wa
　　　露にぬれつつ　　　　　tsuyu ni nuretsutsu

2. 　　持統天皇　　　　　　　Jitō Tennō

　　　春過ぎて　　　　　　　Haru sugite
　　　夏来にけらし　　　　　natsu kinikerashi
　　　白妙の　　　　　　　　shiro-tae no
　　　衣ほすてふ　　　　　　koromo hosu chō
　　　天の香具山　　　　　　ama no kagu-yama

3. 　　柿本人麻呂　　　　　　Kakinomoto no Hitomaro

　　　あしびきの　　　　　　Ashi-biki no
　　　山鳥の尾の　　　　　　yama-dori no o no
　　　しだり尾の　　　　　　shidari-o no
　　　ながながし夜を　　　　naga-nagashi yo wo
　　　ひとりかも寝む　　　　hitori kamo nen

4. 山部赤人　　　　　　　　　Yamabe no Akahito

　　田子の浦に　　　　　　　Tago no ura ni
　　うちいでて見れば　　　　uchi-idete mireba
　　白妙の　　　　　　　　　shiro-tae no
　　富士の高嶺に　　　　　　fuji no taka-ne ni
　　雪はふりつつ　　　　　　yuki wa furitsutsu

5. 猿丸大夫　　　　　　　　　Sarumaru Dayū

　　奥山に　　　　　　　　　Oku-yama ni
　　紅葉踏みわけ　　　　　　momiji fumi-wake
　　鳴く鹿の　　　　　　　　naku shika no
　　声きく時ぞ　　　　　　　koe kiku toki zo
　　秋はかなしき　　　　　　aki wa kanashiki

6. 大伴家持　　　　　　　　　Ōtomo no Yakamochi

　　かささぎの　　　　　　　Kasasagi no
　　渡せる橋に　　　　　　　wataseru hashi ni
　　おく霜の　　　　　　　　oku shimo no
　　白きを見れば　　　　　　shiroki wo mireba
　　夜ぞふけにける　　　　　yo zo fukenikeru

7. 安倍仲麿　　　　　　　　　Abe no Nakamaro

　　天の原　　　　　　　　　Ama no hara
　　ふりさけ見れば　　　　　furi-sake-mireba
　　春日なる　　　　　　　　kasuga naru
　　三笠の山に　　　　　　　mikasa no yama ni
　　出でし月かも　　　　　　ideshi tsuki kamo

8. 喜撰法師　　　　　　　　　Kisen Hōshi

　　わが庵は　　　　　　　　Wa ga io wa
　　都のたつみ　　　　　　　miyako no tatsu-mi
　　しかぞ住む　　　　　　　shika zo sumu
　　世をうぢ山と　　　　　　yo wo uji-yama to
　　人はいふなり　　　　　　hito wa iu nari

Waka and Romanized Transliteration of Waka 157

9. 小野小町   Ono no Komachi

　花の色は   Hana no iro wa
　うつりにけりな   utsurinikeri na
　いたづらに   itazura ni
　わが身よにふる   wa ga mi yo ni furu
　ながめせしまに   nagame seshi ma ni

10. 蝉丸   Semimaru

　これやこの   Kore ya kono
　行くも帰るも   yuku mo kaeru mo
　別れては   wakaretewa
　知るも知らぬも   shiru mo shiranu mo
　逢坂の関   osaka no seki

11. 小野篁   Ono no Takamura

　わたの原   Wata no hara
　八十島かけて   yaso shima kakete
　漕ぎ出でぬと   kogi-idenu to
　人には告げよ   hito ni wa tsugeyo
　海女の釣舟   ama no tsuri-bune

12. 僧正遍照   Sōjō Henjō

　天つ風   Amatsu kaze
　雲の通ひ路   kumo no kayoi-ji
　吹きとぢよ   fuki-tojiyo
　をとめの姿   otome no sugata
　しばしとどめむ   shibashi todomen

13. 陽成院   Yōzei In

　筑波嶺の   Tsukuba-ne no
　峰より落つる   mine yori otsuru
　みなの川   minano gawa
　恋ぞつもりて   koi zo tsumorite
　淵となりぬる   fuchi to narinuru

14. 源融　　　　　　　　　Minamoto no Tōru

　　陸奥の　　　　　　　　Michinoku no
　　しのぶもぢずり　　　　shinobu moji-zuri
　　誰ゆゑに　　　　　　　tare yue ni
　　乱れそめにし　　　　　midare-somenishi
　　我ならなくに　　　　　ware naranaku ni

15. 光孝天皇　　　　　　　Kōkō Tennō

　　君がため　　　　　　　Kimi ga tame
　　春の野に出でて　　　　haru no no ni idete
　　若菜つむ　　　　　　　waka-na tsumu
　　我が衣手に　　　　　　wa ga koromo-de ni
　　雪は降りつつ　　　　　yuki wa furitsutsu

16. 在原行平　　　　　　　Ariwara no Yukihira

　　立ち別れ　　　　　　　Tachi-wakare
　　いなばの山の　　　　　inaba no yama no
　　峰に生ふる　　　　　　mine ni ouru
　　まつとし聞かば　　　　matsu to shi kikaba
　　今帰り来む　　　　　　ima kaeri-kon

17. 在原業平　　　　　　　Ariwara no Narihira

　　ちはやぶる　　　　　　Chihayaburu
　　神代も聞かず　　　　　kami-yo mo kikazu
　　竜田川　　　　　　　　tatsuta-gawa
　　からくれなゐに　　　　kara-kurenai ni
　　水くぐるとは　　　　　mizu kuguru to wa

18. 藤原敏行　　　　　　　Fujiwara no Toshiyuki

　　住の江の　　　　　　　Suminoe no
　　岸に寄る波　　　　　　kishi ni yoru nami
　　よるさへや　　　　　　yoru sae ya
　　夢の通ひ路　　　　　　yume no kayoi-ji
　　人目よくらむ　　　　　hitome yokuran

19.	伊勢	Ise
	難波潟 みじかき蘆の ふしの間も 逢はでこの世を 過ぐしてよとや	Naniwa-gata mijikaki ashi no fushi no ma mo awade kono yo wo sugushiteyo to ya
20.	元良親王	Motoyoshi Shinnō
	わびぬれば 今はた同じ 難波なる みをつくしても 逢はむとぞ思ふ	Wabinureba ima hata onaji naniwa naru miwotsukushite mo awan to zo omou
21.	素性法師	Sosei Hōshi
	今来むと 言ひしばかりに 長月の 有明の月を 待ち出でつるかな	Ima kon to iishi bakari ni naga-tsuki no ariake no tsuki wo machi-idetsuru kana
22.	文屋康秀	Fun'ya (Bun'ya) no Yasuhide
	吹くからに 秋の草木の しをるれば むべ山風を 嵐といふらむ	Fuku kara ni aki no kusaki no shiorureba mube yama-kaze wo arashi to iuran
23.	大江千里	Ōe no Chisato
	月みれば ちぢに物こそ 悲しけれ わが身ひとつの 秋にはあらねど	Tsuki mireba chi-ji ni mono koso kanashikere wa ga mi hitotsu no aki ni wa aranedo

24. 菅原道真　　　　　　　Sugawara no Michizane

　　このたびは　　　　　　Kono tabi wa
　　ぬさもとりあへず　　　nusa mo tori-aezu
　　手向山　　　　　　　　tamuke-yama
　　紅葉の錦　　　　　　　momiji no nishiki
　　神のまにまに　　　　　kami no mani-mani

25. 藤原定方　　　　　　　Fujiwara no Sadakata

　　名にしおはば　　　　　Na ni shi owaba
　　逢坂山の　　　　　　　osaka-yama no
　　さねかづら　　　　　　sanekazura
　　人にしられで　　　　　hito ni shirarede
　　くるよしもがな　　　　kuru yoshi mogana

26. 藤原忠平　　　　　　　Fujiwara no Tadahira

　　小倉山　　　　　　　　Ogura-yama
　　峰のもみじば　　　　　mine no momiji-ba
　　心あらば　　　　　　　kokoro araba
　　今ひとたびの　　　　　ima hito-tabi no
　　みゆき待たなむ　　　　mi-yuki matanan

27. 藤原兼輔　　　　　　　Fujiwara no Kanesuke

　　みかの原　　　　　　　Mika no hara
　　わきて流るる　　　　　wakite nagaruru
　　いづみ川　　　　　　　izumi-gawa
　　いつ見きとてか　　　　itsu miki tote ka
　　恋しかるらむ　　　　　koishikaruran

28. 源宗于　　　　　　　　Minamoto no Muneyuki

　　山里は　　　　　　　　Yama-zato wa
　　冬ぞさびしさ　　　　　fuyu zo sabishisa
　　まさりける　　　　　　masarikeru
　　人目も草も　　　　　　hito-me mo kusa mo
　　かれぬと思へば　　　　karenu to omoeba

29. 凡河内躬恒　　　　Ōshikōchi no Mitsune

　　心あてに　　　　　Kokoro-ate ni
　　折らばや折らむ　　oraba ya oran
　　初霜の　　　　　　hatsu-shimo no
　　置きまどはせる　　oki-madowaseru
　　白菊の花　　　　　shira-giku no hana

30. 壬生忠岑　　　　　Mibu no Tadamine

　　有明の　　　　　　Ariake no
　　つれなく見えし　　tsurenaku mieshi
　　別れより　　　　　wakare yori
　　あかつきばかり　　Akatsuki bakari
　　憂きものはなし　　uki mono wa nashi

31. 坂上是則　　　　　Sakanoue no Korenori

　　朝ぼらけ　　　　　Asaborake
　　有明の月と　　　　ariake no tsuki to
　　見るまでに　　　　miru made ni
　　吉野の里に　　　　yoshino no sato ni
　　ふれる白雪　　　　fureru shira-yuki

32. 春道列樹　　　　　Harumichi no Tsuraki

　　山川に　　　　　　Yama-gawa ni
　　風のかけたる　　　kaze no kaketaru
　　しがらみは　　　　shigarami wa
　　流れもあへぬ　　　nagare mo aenu
　　紅葉なりけり　　　momiji narikeri

33. 紀友則　　　　　　Ki no Tomonori

　　ひさかたの　　　　Hisakata no
　　光のどけき　　　　hikari nodokeki
　　春の日に　　　　　haru no hi ni
　　しづ心なく　　　　shizu-kokoro naku
　　花の散るらむ　　　hana no chiruran

Waka and Romanized Transliteration of Waka

34. 藤原興風　　　　　　Fujiwara no Okikaze

　　誰をかも　　　　　　Tare wo ka mo
　　知る人にせむ　　　　shiru hito ni sen
　　高砂の　　　　　　　takasago no
　　松も昔の　　　　　　matsu mo mukashi no
　　友ならなくに　　　　tomo naranaku ni

35. 紀貫之　　　　　　　Ki no Tsurayuki

　　人はいさ　　　　　　Hito wa isa
　　心も知らず　　　　　kokoro mo shirazu
　　ふるさとは　　　　　furu-sato wa
　　花ぞ昔の　　　　　　hana zo mukashi no
　　香ににほひける　　　ka ni nioikeru

36. 清原深養父　　　　　Kiyohara no Fukayabu

　　夏の夜は　　　　　　Natsu no yo wa
　　まだ宵ながら　　　　mada yoi nagara
　　明けぬるを　　　　　akenuru wo
　　雲のいづこに　　　　kumo no izuko ni
　　月やどるらむ　　　　tsuki yadoruran

37. 文屋朝康　　　　　　Fun'ya no Asayasu

　　白露に　　　　　　　Shira-tsuyu ni
　　風の吹きしく　　　　kaze no fuki-shiku
　　秋の野は　　　　　　aki no no wa
　　つらぬきとめぬ　　　tsuranuki-tomenu
　　玉ぞ散りける　　　　tama zo chirikeru

38. 右近　　　　　　　　Ukon

　　忘らるる　　　　　　Wasuraruru
　　身をば思はず　　　　mi woba omowazu
　　誓ひてし　　　　　　chikaiteshi
　　人の命の　　　　　　hito no inochi no
　　惜しくもあるかな　　oshiku mo aru kana

39.	源等		Minamoto no Hitoshi
	浅茅生の		Asajiu no
	小野の篠原		ono no shinohara
	しのぶれど		shinoburedo
	あまりてなどか		amarite nado ka
	人の恋しき		hito no koishiki
40.	平兼盛		Taira no Kanemori
	しのぶれど		Shinoburedo
	色に出でにけり		iro ni idenikeri
	我が恋は		wa ga koi wa
	物や思ふと		mono ya omou to
	人の問ふまで		hito no tou made
41.	壬生忠見		Mibu no Tadami
	恋すてふ		Koi su chō
	わが名はまだき		wa ga na wa madaki
	立ちにけり		tachinikeri
	人知れずこそ		hito shirezu koso
	思ひそめしか		omoi-someshika
42.	清原元輔		Kiyohara no Motosuke
	契りきな		Chigiriki na
	かたみに袖を		katami ni sode wo
	しぼりつつ		shiboritsutsu
	末の松山		sue no matsu-yama
	波越さじとは		nami kosaji to wa
43.	藤原敦忠		Fujiwara no Atsutada
	逢ひ見ての		Ai-mite no
	のちの心に		nochi no kokoro ni
	くらぶれば		kurabureba
	昔はものを		mukashi wa mono wo
	思はざりけり		omowazarikeri

44. 藤原朝忠　　　　　　　Fujiwara no Asatada

　　逢ふことの　　　　　　Au koto no
　　絶えてしなくは　　　　taete shi naku wa
　　なかなかに　　　　　　naka-naka ni
　　人をも身をも　　　　　hito wo mo mi wo mo
　　恨みざらまし　　　　　uramizaramashi

45. 藤原伊尹　　　　　　　Fujiwara no Koremasa

　　あはれとも　　　　　　Aware to mo
　　いふべき人は　　　　　iu-beki hito wa
　　思ほえで　　　　　　　omooede
　　身のいたづらに　　　　mi no itazura ni
　　なりぬべきかな　　　　narinu-beki kana

46. 曽禰好忠　　　　　　　Sone no Yoshitada

　　由良のとを　　　　　　Yura no to wo
　　渡る舟人　　　　　　　wataru funa-bito
　　かぢをたえ　　　　　　kaji-wo tae
　　行方も知らぬ　　　　　yukue mo shiranu
　　恋の道かな　　　　　　koi no michi kana

47. 恵慶法師　　　　　　　Egyō Hōshi

　　八重むぐら　　　　　　Yae mugura
　　しげれる宿の　　　　　shigereru yado no
　　さびしきに　　　　　　sabishiki ni
　　人こそ見えね　　　　　hito koso miene
　　秋は来にけり　　　　　aki wa kinikeri

48. 源重之　　　　　　　　Minamoto no Shigeyuki

　　風をいたみ　　　　　　Kaze wo itami
　　岩うつ波の　　　　　　iwa utsu nami no
　　おのれのみ　　　　　　onore nomi
　　くだけてものを　　　　kudakete mono wo
　　思ふころかな　　　　　omou koro kana

49.	大中臣能宣	Ōnakatomi no Yoshinobu
	みかきもり	Mi-kaki-mori
	衛士のたく火の	eji no taku hi no
	夜は燃え	yoru wa moe
	昼は消えつつ	hiru wa kietsutsu
	ものをこそ思へ	mono wo koso omoe
50.	藤原義孝	Fujiwara no Yoshitaka
	君がため	Kimi ga tame
	惜しからざりし	oshikarazarishi
	命さへ	inochi sae
	長くもがなと	nagaku mogana to
	思ひぬるかな	omoinuru kana
51.	藤原実方	Fujiwara no Sanekata
	かくとだに	Kaku to dani
	えやはいぶきの	e ya wa ibuki no
	さしも草	sashimo-gusa
	さしも知らじな	sa shimo shiraji na
	燃ゆる思ひを	moyuru omoi wo
52.	藤原道信	Fujiwara no Michinobu
	明けぬれば	Akenureba
	暮るるものとは	kururu mono to wa
	知りながら	shiri-nagara
	なほうらめしき	nao urameshiki
	朝ぼらけかな	asaborake kana
53.	右大将道綱母	Udaishō Michitsuna no Haha
	嘆きつつ	Nagekitsutsu
	ひとり寝る夜の	hitori nuru yo no
	明くる間は	akuru ma wa
	いかに久しき	ika ni hisashiki
	ものとかは知る	mono to ka wa shiru

54. 儀同三司母　　　　　Gitōsanshi no Haha

　　忘れじの　　　　　　Wasureji no
　　行く末までは　　　　yuku-sue made wa
　　かたければ　　　　　katakereba
　　今日を限りの　　　　kyou wo kagiri no
　　命ともがな　　　　　inochi to mogana

55. 藤原公任　　　　　　Fujiwara no Kintō

　　滝の音は　　　　　　Taki no oto wa
　　絶えて久しく　　　　taete hisashiku
　　なりぬれど　　　　　narinuredo
　　名こそ流れて　　　　na koso nagarete
　　なほ聞こえけれ　　　nao kikoekere

56. 和泉式部　　　　　　Izumi Shikibu

　　あらざらむ　　　　　Arazaran
　　この世のほかの　　　kono yo no hoka no
　　思ひ出に　　　　　　omoide ni
　　今ひとたびの　　　　ima hito-tabi no
　　逢ふこともがな　　　au koto mogana

57. 紫式部　　　　　　　Murasaki Shikibu

　　めぐり逢ひて　　　　Meguri-aite
　　見しやそれとも　　　mishi ya sore tomo
　　わかぬ間に　　　　　wakanu ma ni
　　雲がくれにし　　　　kumo-gakurenishi
　　夜半の月かな　　　　yowa no tsuki-kana

58. 大弐三位　　　　　　Daini no Sanmi

　　有馬山　　　　　　　Arima-yama
　　猪名の笹原　　　　　ina no sasahara
　　風吹けば　　　　　　kaze fukeba
　　いでそよ人を　　　　ide soyo hito wo
　　忘れやはする　　　　wasure ya wa suru

59. 赤染衛門　　　　　　　Akazome Emon

　　やすらはで　　　　　　Yasurawade
　　寝なましものを　　　　nenamashi mono wo
　　さ夜ふけて　　　　　　sayo fukete
　　かたぶくまでの　　　　katabuku made no
　　月を見しかな　　　　　tsuki wo mishi kana

60. 小式部内侍　　　　　　Koshikibu no Naishi

　　大江山　　　　　　　　Ōe-yama
　　いく野の道の　　　　　ikuno no michi no
　　遠ければ　　　　　　　tookereba
　　まだふみもみず　　　　mada fumi mo mizu
　　天の橋立　　　　　　　ama no hashidate

61. 伊勢大輔　　　　　　　Ise no Taifu

　　いにしへの　　　　　　Inishie no
　　奈良の都の　　　　　　Nara no miyako no
　　八重桜　　　　　　　　yae-zakura
　　けふ九重に　　　　　　kyō kokonoe ni
　　にほひぬるかな　　　　nioinuru kana

62. 清少納言　　　　　　　Sei Shōnagon

　　夜をこめて　　　　　　Yo wo komete
　　鳥のそらねは　　　　　tori no sora-ne wa
　　はかるとも　　　　　　hakaru tomo
　　よに逢坂の　　　　　　yo ni osaka no
　　関はゆるさじ　　　　　seki wa yurusaji

63. 藤原道雅　　　　　　　Fujiwara no Michimasa

　　今はただ　　　　　　　Ima wa tada
　　思ひ絶えなむ　　　　　omoi-taenan
　　とばかりを　　　　　　to bakari wo
　　人づてならで　　　　　hito-zute narade
　　言ふよしもがな　　　　iu yoshi mogana

64. 藤原定頼　　　　　　　Fujiwara no Sadayori

　　朝ぼらけ　　　　　　　Asaborake
　　宇治の川霧　　　　　　uji no kawa-giri
　　たえだえに　　　　　　tae-dae ni
　　あらはれわたる　　　　araware-wataru
　　瀬々の網代木　　　　　se-ze no ajiro-gi

65. 相模　　　　　　　　　Sagami

　　恨みわび　　　　　　　Urami-wabi
　　ほさぬ袖だに　　　　　hosanu sode dani
　　あるものを　　　　　　aru mono wo
　　恋に朽ちなむ　　　　　koi ni kuchinan
　　名こそ惜しけれ　　　　na koso oshikere

66. 前大僧正行尊　　　　　Saki no Dai Sōjō Gyōson

　　もろともに　　　　　　Morotomo ni
　　あはれと思へ　　　　　aware to omoe
　　山桜　　　　　　　　　yama-zakura
　　花よりほかに　　　　　hana yori hoka ni
　　知る人もなし　　　　　shiru hito mo nashi

67. 周防内侍　　　　　　　Suō no Naishi

　　春の夜の　　　　　　　Haru no yo no
　　夢ばかりなる　　　　　yume bakari naru
　　手枕に　　　　　　　　ta-makura ni
　　かひなく立たむ　　　　kai naku tatan
　　名こそ惜しけれ　　　　na koso oshikere

68. 三条院　　　　　　　　Sanjō In

　　心にも　　　　　　　　Kokoro ni mo
　　あらでうき世に　　　　arade uki yo ni
　　ながらへば　　　　　　nagaraeba
　　恋しかるべき　　　　　koishikarubeki
　　夜半の月かな　　　　　yowa no tsuki kana

69.	能因法師	Nōin Hōshi
	嵐吹く	Arashi fuku
	三室の山の	mimuro no yama no
	もみぢ葉は	momiji-ba wa
	竜田の川の	tatsuta no kawa no
	錦なりけり	nishiki narikeri
70.	良暹法師	Ryōzen Hōshi
	さびしさに	Sabishisa ni
	宿をたち出でて	yado wo tachi-idete
	ながむれば	nagamureba
	いづくも同じ	izuku mo onaji
	秋の夕暮れ	aki no yuugure
71.	源経信	Minamoto no Tsunenobu
	夕されば	Yū sareba
	門田の稲葉	kado-ta no inaba
	おとづれて	otozurete
	芦のまろやに	ashi no maro-ya ni
	秋風ぞ吹く	aki-kaze zo fuku
72.	祐子内親王家紀伊	Yūshi Naishinnō-ke no Kii
	音に聞く	Oto ni kiku
	高師の浜の	takashi no hama no
	あだ波は	ada-nami wa
	かけじや袖の	kakeji ya sode no
	ぬれもこそすれ	nure mo koso sure
73.	大江匡房	Ōe no Masafusa
	高砂の	Takasago no
	尾の上の桜	onoe no sakura
	咲きにけり	sakinikeri
	外山の霞	toyama no kasumi
	立たずもあらなむ	tatazu mo aranan

74. 源俊頼 — Minamoto no Toshiyori

憂かりける　　　　　Ukarikeru
人を初瀬の　　　　　hito wo hatsuse no
山おろしよ　　　　　yama-oroshiyo
はげしかれとは　　　hageshikare to wa
祈らぬものを　　　　inoranu mono wo

75. 藤原基俊 — Fujiwara no Mototoshi

契りおきし　　　　　Chigiri-okishi
させもが露を　　　　sasemo ga tsuyu wo
命にて　　　　　　　inochi nite
あはれ今年の　　　　aware kotoshi no
秋もいぬめり　　　　aki mo inumeri

76. 藤原忠通 — Fujiwara no Tadamichi

わたの原　　　　　　Wata no hara
漕ぎ出でて見れば　　kogi-idete mireba
ひさかたの　　　　　hisakata no
雲居にまがふ　　　　kumoi ni magau
沖つ白波　　　　　　okitsu shiranami

77. 崇徳院 — Sutoku In

瀬をはやみ　　　　　Se wo hayami
岩にせかるる　　　　iwa ni sekaruru
滝川の　　　　　　　taki-gawa no
われても末に　　　　warete mo sue ni
あはむとぞ思ふ　　　awan to zo omou

78. 源兼昌 — Minamoto no Kanemasa

淡路島　　　　　　　Awaji shima
かよふ千鳥の　　　　kayou chidori no
鳴く声に　　　　　　naku koe ni
いく夜寝覚めぬ　　　iku yo ne-zamenu
須磨の関守　　　　　suma no seki-mori

79.　藤原顕輔　　　　　　　Fujiwara no Akisuke

　　　秋風に　　　　　　　　Aki-kaze ni
　　　たなびく雲の　　　　　tanabiku kumo no
　　　絶え間より　　　　　　tae-ma yori
　　　もれ出づる月の　　　　more-izuru tsuki no
　　　影のさやけさ　　　　　kage no sayakesa

80.　待賢門院堀河　　　　　Taikenmon In Horikawa

　　　長からむ　　　　　　　Nagakaran
　　　心も知らず　　　　　　kokoro mo shirazu
　　　黒髪の　　　　　　　　kuro-kami no
　　　乱れて今朝は　　　　　midarete kesa wa
　　　ものをこそ思へ　　　　mono wo koso omoe

81.　藤原実定　　　　　　　Fujiwara no Sanesada

　　　ほととぎす　　　　　　Hototogisu
　　　鳴きつる方を　　　　　nakitsuru kata wo
　　　ながむれば　　　　　　nagamureba
　　　ただ有明の　　　　　　tada ariake no
　　　月ぞ残れる　　　　　　tsuki zo nokoreru

82.　道因法師　　　　　　　Dōin Hōshi

　　　思ひわび　　　　　　　Omoi-wabi
　　　さても命は　　　　　　sate mo inochi wa
　　　あるものを　　　　　　aru monowo
　　　憂きにたへぬは　　　　uki ni taenu wa
　　　涙なりけり　　　　　　namida nari keri

83.　藤原俊成　　　　　　　Fujiwara no Toshinari

　　　世の中よ　　　　　　　Yo no naka yo
　　　道こそなけれ　　　　　michi koso nakere
　　　思ひ入る　　　　　　　omoi-iru
　　　山の奥にも　　　　　　yama no oku ni mo
　　　鹿ぞ鳴くなる　　　　　shika zo naku naru

84. 藤原清輔　　　　　　　Fujiwara no Kiyosuke

　　ながらへば　　　　　　Nagaraeba
　　またこのごろや　　　　mata kono goro ya
　　しのばれむ　　　　　　shinobaren
　　憂しとみし世ぞ　　　　ushi to mishi yo zo
　　今は恋しき　　　　　　ima wa koishiki

85. 俊恵法師　　　　　　　Shun'e Hōshi

　　夜もすがら　　　　　　Yomosugara
　　もの思ふころは　　　　mono-omou koro wa
　　明けやらで　　　　　　akeyarade
　　閨のひまさへ　　　　　neya no hima sae
　　つれなかりけり　　　　tsurenakarikeri

86. 西行法師　　　　　　　Saigyō Hōshi

　　嘆けとて　　　　　　　Nageke tote
　　月やはものを　　　　　tsuki ya wa mono wo
　　思はする　　　　　　　omowasuru
　　かこち顔なる　　　　　kakochi-gao naru
　　わが涙かな　　　　　　wa ga namida kana

87. 寂蓮法師　　　　　　　Jakuren Hōshi

　　村雨の　　　　　　　　Murasame no
　　露もまだひぬ　　　　　tsuyu mo mada hinu
　　まきの葉に　　　　　　maki no ha ni
　　霧たちのぼる　　　　　kiri tachi-noboru
　　秋の夕暮れ　　　　　　aki no yuu-gure

88. 皇嘉門院別当　　　　　Kōkamon In no Bettō

　　難波江の　　　　　　　Naniwa-e no
　　芦のかりねの　　　　　ashi no kari-ne no
　　ひとよゆゑ　　　　　　hito-yo yue
　　みをつくしてや　　　　miwotsukushite ya
　　恋ひわたるべき　　　　koi-wataru-beki

89. 式子内親王   Shokushi Naishinnō

     玉の緒よ   Tama no o yo
     絶えなば絶えね   taenaba taene
     ながらへば   nagaraeba
     忍ぶることの   shinoburu koto no
     よわりもぞする   yowari mo zo suru

90. 殷富門院大輔   Inpumon In no Taifu

     見せばやな   Misebaya na
     雄島のあまの   ojima no ama no
     袖だにも   sode dani mo
     ぬれにぞぬれし   nure ni zo nureshi
     色はかはらず   iro wa kawarazu

91. 藤原良経   Fujiwara no Yoshitsune

     きりぎりす   Kirigirisu
     鳴くや霜夜の   naku ya shimo-yo no
     さむしろに   sa-mushiro ni
     衣かたしき   koromo kata-shiki
     ひとりかも寝む   hitori ka mo nen

92. 二条院讃岐   Nijō In no Sanuki

     わが袖は   Wa ga sode wa
     潮干にみえぬ   shiohi ni mienu
     沖の石の   oki no ishi no
     人こそ知らね   hito koso shirane
     乾く間もなし   kawaku ma mo nashi

93. 源実朝   Minamoto no Sanetomo

     世の中は   Yo no naka wa
     常にもがもな   tsune ni mogamo na
     渚こぐ   nagisa kogu
     あまの小舟の   ama no o-bune no
     綱手かなしも   tsunade kanashi mo

94. 藤原雅経　　　　　　Fujiwara no Masatsune

　　み吉野の　　　　　　Mi-yoshino no
　　山の秋風　　　　　　yama no aki-kaze
　　さ夜ふけて　　　　　sa-yo fukete
　　ふるさと寒く　　　　furu-sato samuku
　　衣うつなり　　　　　koromo utsu nari

95. 前大僧正慈円　　　　Saki no Dai Sōjō Jien

　　おほけなく　　　　　Ōke naku
　　うき世の民に　　　　uki yo no tami ni
　　おほふかな　　　　　ōu kana
　　わがたつ杣に　　　　wa ga tatsu soma ni
　　墨染の袖　　　　　　sumi-zome no sode

96. 藤原公経　　　　　　Fujiwara no Kintsune

　　花さそふ　　　　　　Hana sasou
　　嵐の庭の　　　　　　arashi no niwa no
　　雪ならで　　　　　　yuki narade
　　ふりゆくものは　　　furi-yuku mono wa
　　わが身なりけり　　　wa ga mi narikeri

97. 藤原定家　　　　　　Fujiwara no Teika (Sadaie)

　　来ぬ人を　　　　　　Konu hito wo
　　まつほの浦の　　　　matsuho no ura no
　　夕なぎに　　　　　　yuu-nagi ni
　　焼くや藻塩の　　　　yaku ya mo-shio no
　　身もこがれつつ　　　mi mo kogaretsutsu

98. 藤原家隆　　　　　　Fujiwara no Ietaka

　　風そよぐ　　　　　　Kaze soyogu
　　ならの小川の　　　　nara no o-gawa no
　　夕暮れは　　　　　　yuu-gure wa
　　みそぎぞ夏の　　　　misogi zo natsu no
　　しるしなりける　　　shirushi narikeru

99. 後鳥羽院　　　　　　　　Gotoba In

　　人もをし　　　　　　　　Hito mo oshi
　　人もうらめし　　　　　　hito mo urameshi
　　あぢきなく　　　　　　　ajikinaku
　　世を思ふゆゑに　　　　　yo wo omou yue ni
　　もの思ふ身は　　　　　　mono-omou mi wa

100. 順徳院　　　　　　　　　Juntoku In

　　ももしきや　　　　　　　Momoshiki ya
　　古き軒端の　　　　　　　furuki noki-ba no
　　しのぶにも　　　　　　　shinobu ni mo
　　なほあまりある　　　　　nao amari aru
　　昔なりけり　　　　　　　mukashi narikeri

GLOSSARY

Engo (verbal association)   Establishment of interrelationships in meaning, sound, and words, especially through word play. These relationships are mostly internal, but sometimes editors of collections place individual poems by different poets in the same collection in "engotic" relationships. The Japanese language is incredibly rich in homonyms and double meanings, making translation a greater challenge. Ono no Komachi was one of the greatest masters of this technique, and poem 9 is a masterpiece of "engotic" relationships. Writing of Komachi, Helen McCullough notes in particular that *engo* is "capable not only of supplying wit, but also of creating romantic, melancholy overtones, which were almost invariably achieved through the association of human feeling with the world of nature" (*Brocade by Night "Kokin Wakashū" and the Court Style in Japanese Classical Poetry*, 350).

Honka-dori (allusive variation)   Adaptation or echoing of words, situation, conception of a poem, or the making new of an older, especially famous, *waka*. Normally requires an actual citation of words from an earlier poem. At its most accomplished, both recognizable elements appear in the poem, but one also feels it is completely new or original. For example, poem 94 on fulling is based on a previous *waka*. By changing the season of the original poem from winter to autumn and from piling up snow to the sound of fulling, the poet has made an old poem completely new.

Kakekotoba (pillow word)   A word or part of a word that is employed in two or sometimes even three ways, one being to refer back to what has preceded and two being to refer to what follows. *Nagame* in poem 9 means both "to look out on" and "long rain." *Matsu* in poem 16 is an example easy to understand in English as it contains exactly the same meanings as used in the translation, namely, "pine tree" and "to pine."

Kashū (private collection)   A private collection of *waka*.

Kotobagaki (headnote)   Note appearing in the text where the poems first appear that describes the circumstances in which the poem was composed. Some headnotes merely give the topic (*dai*), but others provide long, detailed accounts, sometimes fictional.

Makura kotoba (pillow word)   Conventional epithets or attributes for a word. Often, the meaning is not completely clear. *Ashibiki*—the pillow word for "mountain"—in poem 3 is one of the most famous examples. The meaning is unclear, but it is usually translated as "foot-dragging" or "wearying." The closest equivalent to this in English is the fixed epithet.

Renga (linked poetry)   Developed in the twelfth century, first, as a pastime and, later, as a serious art form. Linked poetry was made up of a succession of linked stanzas of 5-7-5 (*kami no ku*) and 7-7 (*shimo no ku*) syllables, respectively, joined into an integral poetic unit and could be of various lengths. They were usually composed by varying numbers of people, typically of one to three (Minor and Morrell, *Princeton Companion to Classical Japanese Literature*, 294).

Tanka (short poem)   A poem of thirty-one syllables in five lines: 5, 7, 5, 7, 7. In classical Japanese, the word *tanka* is used to indicate only the short poem acting as an envoy to long poems (*chōka*). Other appearances of poems in the same form are always referred to as *waka* or *uta* (song). *Waka* can refer to both court poetry and Japanese poetry in general, including *chōka*, *katauta*, *sedōka*, *renga*, and *haiku*. Since the Meiji period *tanka* refers to poems in the short form with relaxed rules, other than those entered for the New Year Poetry Reading Ceremony (*utakai hajime*) at the court, which are still called *waka*.

BIBLIOGRAPHY

English-Language Works

Bly, Robert. *The Eight Stages of Translation.* Boston: Rowan Tree Press, 1986.

Brower, Robert H., and Earl Miner. *Fujiwara Teika's Superior Poems of Our Time.* Stanford: Stanford University Press, 1967.

Bundy, Roselee. "Solo Poetry Contest as Poetic Self-Portrait: The One-Hundred-Round Contest of Lord Teika's Own Poems (1)." *Monumenta Nipponica* 61:1 (Spring 2006):1–58.

———. "Solo Poetry Contest as Poetic Self-Portrait: The One-Hundred-Round Contest of Lord Teika's Own Poems (2)." *Monumenta Nipponica* 61:2 (Summer 2006):131–192.

Cranston, Edwin A., trans. *A Waka Anthology, Volume Two: Grasses of Remembrance.* Stanford: Stanford University Press, 2006.

Fujiwara no Teika. *Maigetsushō.* Trans. Toshihiko and Toyo Izutsu. In *The Theory of Beauty in the Classical Aesthetics of Japan,* pp. 79–96. The Hague, Boston, London: Martinus Nijhoff, 1981.

———. *Superior Poems of Our Time. Kindai Shūka.* Trans. Robert H. Brower and Earl Miner. Stanford: Stanford University Press, 1967.

Keene, Donald. *Japanese Literature (An Introduction for Western Readers).* Tokyo: Charles E. Tuttle, 1977.

———. *Seeds in the Heart: Japanese Literature from Earliest Times to the Late Sixteenth Century.* New York: Henry Holt, 1993.

——. *The Pleasures of Japanese Literature.* New York: Columbia University Press, 1988.

Kenkō. *Essays in Idleness (Tsurezuregusa).* Trans. Donald Keene. Tokyo: Charles E. Tuttle, 1981.

Konishi Jin'ichi. *A History of Japanese Literature*, Vol. 3: *The High Middle Ages.* Trans. Aileen Gatten and Mark Harbison. Princeton: Princeton University Press, 1991.

McCullough, Helen Craig. *Brocade by Night "Kokin Wakashū" and the Court Style in Japanese Classical Poetry.* Stanford: Stanford University Press, 1985.

——. *Kokin Wakashū with "Tosa Nikki" and "Shinsen Waka."* Stanford: Stanford University Press, 1985.

——. *Tale of the Heike.* Stanford: Stanford University Press, 1988.

——. *Tales of Ise (Ise Monogatari).* Stanford: Stanford University Press, 1968.

Miner, Earl. *An Introduction to Japanese Court Poetry.* Stanford: Stanford University Press, 1968.

Miner, Earl, Hiroko Odagiri, and Robert E. Morrell. *The Princeton Companion to Classical Japanese Literature.* Princeton: Princeton University Press, 1958.

Mostow, Joshua. *Pictures of the Heart.* Honolulu: University of Hawai'i Press, 1996.

Murasaki Shikibu. *The Tale of Genji (Genji Monogatari).* Trans. Royall Tyler. New York: Viking Penguin, 2001

Rexroth, Kenneth. *One Hundred Poems from the Japanese.* New York: New Directions, 1964.

Schulte, Rainer, and John Biguenet. *Theories of Translation.* Chicago: University of Chicago Press, 1992.

Sōgi. "Pilgrimage to Dazaifu" (*Tsukushi no Michi no Ki*). Trans. Eileen Kato. *Monumenta Nipponica* 34:3 (Autumn 1979):333–367.

Stewart, Frank. *The Poem Behind the Poem: Translating Asian Poetry.* Washington, DC: Copper Canyon Press, 2004.

Tsumura Kimiko. "The Love Letters" (*Fumigara*). In *Ono no Komachi: Poems, Stories, No Plays*, pp. 211–220. Trans. Roy E. Teele, Nicholas Teele, and H. Rebecca Teele. New York: Garland, 1993.

Ukon. *Tales of Yamato*. Trans. Mildred Tahara. Honolulu: University of Hawai'i Press, 1980.
Waley, Arthur. *Japanese Poetry, the "Uta"*. Oxford: Clarendon Press, 1919.
Wheelwright, Carolyn. *Word in Flower: The Visualization of Classical Literature in Seventeenth-Century Japan.* New Haven: Yale University Art Gallery, 1989.

Japanese-Language Works

Anno Hideko. *Hito ni Hanasitakunaru Hyakunin Isshu.* Tokyo: Poplar, 2004.
Inoue Muneo. *Hyakunin Isshu (Ōchō Waka kara Chūsei Waka e)*. Tokyo: Kasama Shoin, 2004.
Inukai Kiyoshi et al., eds. *Waka Daijiten*. Tokyo: Meijishoin, 1986.
Katagiri Yōichi. *Utamakura Utakotoba Jiten*. Tokyo: Kasama Shoin, 1999.
Kubota Jun and Baba Akiko, eds. *Utakotoba Utamakura Daijiten*. Tokyo: Kadokawa Shoten, 1999.
Nakagawa Hirofumi and Yukinobu Miki. *Shin Ogura Hyakunin Isshu.* Kyoto: Kyoto Shobo, 1995.
Ōoka Makoto. *Hyakunin Isshu*. Tokyo: Sekai Bunka, 2005.
Satō Yasushi. *Eiri Hyakunin Isshu Nyūmon.* Tokyo: Tsuchiya Shoten, 2005.
Shimazu Tadao, ed. *Hyakunin Isshu.* Tokyo: Kadokawa Shoten, 1969.
Shimazu Tadao and Kamijō Shōji, eds. *Hyakunin Isshu Kochūshō*. Osaka: Izumi Shoin, 1982.
Suzuki Hideo, Yamaguchi Shin'ichi, and Yoda Yasushi. *Genshoku Ogura Hyakunin Isshu.* Tokyo: Bun'ei Dō, 2004.
Takagi Kiyoko. "Hyakunin Isshu to Sono Shūhen." *Uchū-Fū*, no. 256 (November 2006): 22–25.

ILLUSTRATION CREDITS

Calligraphy accompanying each poem. *Hyakunin Isshu* (911.147//HYA// Mori Bunko L-12141). In the hand of Abbot Genchin in 1660 (Manji 3) in the fifth month. (Osaka City University, Media Center)

Line drawings of the 100 poets. *Hyakunin Isshu*. Kuwagata Keisai. Edo period (nineteenth century). (Gifu City Public Library)

Figure 1. Portrait of Fujiwara no Teika. Attributed to Fujiwara no Nobuzane. (Shiguretei, Reizei Family Archive)

Figure 2. *Ogura shikishi*, poem 43 from the anthology *Ogura Hyakunin Isshu*. Calligraphy attributed to Fujiwara no Sadaie (1162–1241). Ink on paper, Kamakura period (thirteenth century). (Gotoh Museum)

Figure 3. *Hyakunin Isshu* playing cards from the middle Edo period. Woodblock print with hand-painting. Calligraphy by hand. (Collection of Hideji Ōyagi)

Figure 4. *Tsubaki ni yuki zu*. Poem (*Shin Kokin Wakashū*, no. 1034) (89 in the *Hyakunin Isshu* but with slight variations in the text). Square paper (*shikishi*) with ground painting of camellia covered with snow, by Hon'ami Kōetsu. Painting attributed to Tawaraya Sōtatsu. From the *Shikishijo*, an album of poems from the *Shin Kokin Wakashū*. Calligraphy by Hon'ami Kōetsu (d. c. 1640). 36 leaves in total. Ink and color on paper, Edo period (seventeenth century). (Gotoh Museum)

Figure 5. Hyakunin Isshu playing cards. (Collection of Hideji Ōyagi)

Figure 6. *Kudzu-zu*. Poem (*Shin Kokin Wakashū*, no. 518) (91 in the *Hyakunin Isshu* but with slight variations in the text). Square paper (*shikishi*) with ground painting of kudzu vine. Calligraphy by Hon'ami Kōetsu. Painting attributed to Tawaraya Sōtatsu. From the *Shikishijō*, an album of poems from the *Shin Kokin Wakashū*. Calligraphy by Hon'ami Kōetsu (d. c. 1640). 36 leaves in total. Ink and color on paper, Edo period (seventeenth century). (Gotoh Museum)

Figure 7. A Segment of Teika's *Meigetsuki*. (Shiguretei, Reizei Family Archive)

Figure 8. *Hyakunin Isshu* playing cards. (Collection of Hideji Ōyagi)

OTHER WORKS IN THE COLUMBIA ASIAN STUDIES SERIES

Translations from the Asian Classics

Major Plays of Chikamatsu, tr. Donald Keene 1961.
Four Major Plays of Chikamatsu, tr. Donald Keene. Paperback ed. only. 1961; rev. ed. 1997.
Records of the Grand Historian of China, translated from the Shih chi of Ssu-ma Ch'ien, tr. Burton Watson, 2 vols. 1961.
Instructions for Practical Living and Other Neo-Confucian Writings by Wang Yang-ming, tr. Wing-tsit Chan 1963.
Hsün Tzu: Basic Writings, tr. Burton Watson, paperback ed. only. 1963; rev. ed. 1996.
Chuang Tzu: Basic Writings, tr. Burton Watson, paperback ed. only. 1964; rev. ed. 1996.
The Mahābhārata, tr. Chakravarthi V. Narasimhan. Also in paperback ed. 1965; rev. ed. 1997.
The Manyōshū, Nippon Gakujutsu Shinkōkai edition 1965.
Su Tung-p'o: Selections from a Sung Dynasty Poet, tr. Burton Watson. Also in paperback ed. 1965.
Bhartrihari: Poems, tr. Barbara Stoler Miller. Also in paperback ed. 1967.
Basic Writings of Mo Tzu, Hsün Tzu, and Han Fei Tzu, tr. Burton Watson. Also in separate paperback eds. 1967.

The Awakening of Faith, Attributed to Aśvaghosha, tr. Yoshito S. Hakeda. Also in paperback ed. 1967.
Reflections on Things at Hand: The Neo-Confucian Anthology, comp. Chu Hsi and Lü Tsu-ch'ien, tr. Wing-tsit Chan 1967.
The Platform Sutra of the Sixth Patriarch, tr. Philip B. Yampolsky. Also in paperback ed. 1967.
Essays in Idleness: The Tsurezuregusa of Kenkō, tr. Donald Keene. Also in paperback ed. 1967.
The Pillow Book of Sei Shōnagon, tr. Ivan Morris, 2 vols. 1967.
Two Plays of Ancient India: The Little Clay Cart and the Minister's Seal, tr. J. A. B. van Buitenen 1968.
The Complete Works of Chuang Tzu, tr. Burton Watson 1968.
The Romance of the Western Chamber (Hsi Hsiang chi), tr. S. I. Hsiung. Also in paperback ed. 1968.
The Manyōshū, Nippon Gakujutsu Shinkōkai edition. Paperback ed. only. 1969.
Records of the Historian: Chapters from the Shih chi of Ssu-ma Ch'ien, tr. Burton Watson. Paperback ed. only. 1969.
Cold Mountain: 100 Poems by the T'ang Poet Han-shan, tr. Burton Watson. Also in paperback ed. 1970.
Twenty Plays of the Nō Theatre, ed. Donald Keene. Also in paperback ed. 1970.
Chūshingura: The Treasury of Loyal Retainers, tr. Donald Keene. Also in paperback ed. 1971; rev. ed. 1997.
The Zen Master Hakuin: Selected Writings, tr. Philip B. Yampolsky 1971.
Chinese Rhyme-Prose: Poems in the Fu Form from the Han and Six Dynasties Periods, tr. Burton Watson. Also in paperback ed. 1971.
Kūkai: Major Works, tr. Yoshito S. Hakeda. Also in paperback ed. 1972.
The Old Man Who Does as He Pleases: Selections from the Poetry and Prose of Lu Yu, tr. Burton Watson 1973.
The Lion's Roar of Queen Śrīmālā, tr. Alex and Hideko Wayman 1974.
Courtier and Commoner in Ancient China: Selections from the History of the Former Han by Pan Ku, tr. Burton Watson. Also in paperback ed. 1974.
Japanese Literature in Chinese, vol. 1: *Poetry and Prose in Chinese by Japanese Writers of the Early Period,* tr. Burton Watson 1975.

Japanese Literature in Chinese, vol. 2: *Poetry and Prose in Chinese by Japanese Writers of the Later Period*, tr. Burton Watson 1976.
Scripture of the Lotus Blossom of the Fine Dharma, tr. Leon Hurvitz. Also in paperback ed. 1976.
Love Song of the Dark Lord: Jayadeva's Gītagovinda, tr. Barbara Stoler Miller. Also in paperback ed. Cloth ed. includes critical text of the Sanskrit. 1977; rev. ed. 1997.
Ryōkan: Zen Monk-Poet of Japan, tr. Burton Watson 1977.
Calming the Mind and Discerning the Real: From the Lam rim chen mo of Tso ṇ-kha-pa, tr. Alex Wayman 1978.
The Hermit and the Love-Thief: Sanskrit Poems of Bhartrihari and Bilhaṇa, tr. Barbara Stoler Miller 1978.
The Lute: Kao Ming's P'i-p'a chi, tr. Jean Mulligan. Also in paperback ed. 1980.
A Chronicle of Gods and Sovereigns: Jinnō Shōtōki of Kitabatake Chikafusa, tr. H. Paul Varley 1980.
Among the Flowers: The Hua-chien chi, tr. Lois Fusek 1982.
Grass Hill: Poems and Prose by the Japanese Monk Gensei, tr. Burton Watson 1983.
Doctors, Diviners, and Magicians of Ancient China: Biographies of Fang-shih, tr. Kenneth J. DeWoskin. Also in paperback ed. 1983.
Theater of Memory: The Plays of Kālidāsa, ed. Barbara Stoler Miller. Also in paperback ed. 1984.
The Columbia Book of Chinese Poetry: From Early Times to the Thirteenth Century, ed. and tr. Burton Watson. Also in paperback ed. 1984.
Poems of Love and War: From the Eight Anthologies and the Ten Long Poems of Classical Tamil, tr. A.K. Ramanujan. Also in paperback ed. 1985.
The Bhagavad Gita: Krishna's Counsel in Time of War, tr. Barbara Stoler Miller 1986.
The Columbia Book of Later Chinese Poetry, ed. and tr. Jonathan Chaves. Also in paperback ed. 1986.
The Tso Chuan: Selections from China's Oldest Narrative History, tr. Burton Watson 1989.
Waiting for the Wind: Thirty-six Poets of Japan's Late Medieval Age, tr. Steven Carter 1989.

Selected Writings of Nichiren, ed. Philip B. Yampolsky 1990.
Saigyō, Poems of a Mountain Home, tr. Burton Watson 1990.
The Book of Lieh Tzu: A Classic of the Tao, tr. A.C. Graham. Morningside ed. 1990.
The Tale of an Anklet: An Epic of South India—The Cilappatikāram of Iḷaṅkō Aṭikaḷ, tr. R. Parthasarathy 1993.
Waiting for the Dawn: A Plan for the Prince, tr. with introduction by Wm. Theodore de Bary 1993.
Yoshitsune and the Thousand Cherry Trees: A Masterpiece of the Eighteenth-Century Japanese Puppet Theater, tr., annotated, and with introduction by Stanleigh H. Jones, Jr. 1993.
The Lotus Sutra, tr. Burton Watson. Also in paperback ed. 1993.
The Classic of Changes: A New Translation of the I Ching *as Interpreted by Wang Bi,* tr. Richard John Lynn 1994.
Beyond Spring: Tz'u Poems of the Sung Dynasty, tr. Julie Landau 1994.
The Columbia Anthology of Traditional Chinese Literature, ed. Victor H. Mair 1994.
Scenes for Mandarins: The Elite Theater of the Ming, tr. Cyril Birch 1995.
Letters of Nichiren, ed. Philip B. Yampolsky; tr. Burton Watson et al. 1996.
Unforgotten Dreams: Poems by the Zen Monk Shōtetsu, tr. Steven D. Carter 1997.
The Vimalakirti Sutra, tr. Burton Watson 1997.
Japanese and Chinese Poems to Sing: The Wakan rōei shū, tr. J. Thomas Rimer and Jonathan Chaves 1997.
Breeze Through Bamboo: Kanshi of Ema Saikō, tr. Hiroaki Sato 1998.
A Tower for the Summer Heat, by Li Yu, tr. Patrick Hanan 1998.
Traditional Japanese Theater: An Anthology of Plays, by Karen Brazell 1998.
The Original Analects: Sayings of Confucius and His Successors (0479–0249), by E. Bruce Brooks and A. Taeko Brooks 1998.
The Classic of the Way and Virtue: A New Translation of the Tao-te ching *of Laozi as Interpreted by Wang Bi,* tr. Richard John Lynn 1999.
The Four Hundred Songs of War and Wisdom: An Anthology of Poems from Classical Tamil, The Puṟanāṉūṟu, ed. and tr. George L. Hart and Hank Heifetz 1999.
Original Tao: Inward Training (Nei-yeh) *and the Foundations of Taoist Mysticism,* by Harold D. Roth 1999.

Lao Tzu's Tao Te Ching: *A Translation of the Startling New Documents Found at Guodian,* by Robert G. Henricks 2000.
The Shorter Columbia Anthology of Traditional Chinese Literature, ed. Victor H. Mair 2000.
Mistress and Maid (Jiaohongji), by Meng Chengshun, tr. Cyril Birch 2001.
Chikamatsu: Five Late Plays, tr. and ed. C. Andrew Gerstle 2001.
The Essential Lotus: Selections from the Lotus Sutra, tr. Burton Watson 2002.
Early Modern Japanese Literature: An Anthology, 1600–1900, ed. Haruo Shirane 2002.
The Sound of the Kiss, or The Story That Must Never Be Told: Pingali Suranna's Kalapurnodayamu, tr. Vecheru Narayana Rao and David Shulman 2003.
The Selected Poems of Du Fu, tr. Burton Watson 2003.
Far Beyond the Field: Haiku by Japanese Women, tr. Makoto Ueda 2003.
Just Living: Poems and Prose by the Japanese Monk Tonna, ed. and tr. Steven D. Carter 2003.
Han Feizi: Basic Writings, tr. Burton Watson 2003.
Mozi: Basic Writings, tr. Burton Watson 2003.
Xunzi: Basic Writings, tr. Burton Watson 2003.
Zhuangzi: Basic Writings, tr. Burton Watson 2003.
The Awakening of Faith, Attributed to Aśvaghosha, tr. Yoshito S. Hakeda, introduction by Ryuichi Abe 2005.
The Tales of the Heike, tr. Burton Watson, ed. Haruo Shirane 2006.
Tales of Moonlight and Rain, by Ueda Akinari, tr. with introduction by Anthony H. Chambers 2007.
Traditional Japanese Literature: An Anthology, Beginnings to 1600, ed. Haruo Shirane 2007.
The Philosophy of Qi, by Kaibara Ekken, tr. Mary Evelyn Tucker 2007.

Modern Asian Literature

Modern Japanese Drama: An Anthology, ed. and tr. Ted. Takaya. Also in paperback ed. 1979.
Mask and Sword: Two Plays for the Contemporary Japanese Theater, by Yamazaki Masakazu, tr. J. Thomas Rimer 1980.
Yokomitsu Riichi, Modernist, by Dennis Keene 1980.

Nepali Visions, Nepali Dreams: The Poetry of Laxmiprasad Devkota, tr. David Rubin 1980.

Literature of the Hundred Flowers, vol. 1: *Criticism and Polemics*, ed. Hualing Nieh 1981.

Literature of the Hundred Flowers, vol. 2: *Poetry and Fiction*, ed. Hualing Nieh 1981.

Modern Chinese Stories and Novellas, 1919–1949, ed. Joseph S. M. Lau, C. T. Hsia, and Leo Ou-fan Lee. Also in paperback ed. 1984.

A View by the Sea, by Yasuoka Shōtarō, tr. Kären Wigen Lewis 1984.

Other Worlds: Arishima Takeo and the Bounds of Modern Japanese Fiction, by Paul Anderer 1984.

Selected Poems of Sŏ Chŏngju, tr. with introduction by David R. McCann 1989.

The Sting of Life: Four Contemporary Japanese Novelists, by Van C. Gessel 1989.

Stories of Osaka Life, by Oda Sakunosuke, tr. Burton Watson 1990.

The Bodhisattva, or Samantabhadra, by Ishikawa Jun, tr. with introduction by William Jefferson Tyler 1990.

The Travels of Lao Ts'an, by Liu T'ieh-yün, tr. Harold Shadick. Morningside ed. 1990.

Three Plays by Kōbō Abe, tr. with introduction by Donald Keene 1993.

The Columbia Anthology of Modern Chinese Literature, ed. Joseph S. M. Lau and Howard Goldblatt 1995.

Modern Japanese Tanka, ed. and tr. Makoto Ueda 1996.

Masaoka Shiki: Selected Poems, ed. and tr. Burton Watson 1997.

Writing Women in Modern China: An Anthology of Women's Literature from the Early Twentieth Century, ed. and tr. Amy D. Dooling and Kristina M. Torgeson 1998.

American Stories, by Nagai Kafū, tr. Mitsuko Iriye 2000.

The Paper Door and Other Stories, by Shiga Naoya, tr. Lane Dunlop 2001.

Grass for My Pillow, by Saiichi Maruya, tr. Dennis Keene 2002.

For All My Walking: Free-Verse Haiku of Taneda Santōka, with Excerpts from His Diaries, tr. Burton Watson 2003.

The Columbia Anthology of Modern Japanese Literature, vol. 1: *From Restoration to Occupation, 1868–1945*, ed. J. Thomas Rimer and Van C. Gessel 2005.

The Columbia Anthology of Modern Japanese Literature, vol. 2: *From 1945 to the Present*, ed. J. Thomas Rimer and Van C. Gessel 2007.

Studies in Asian Culture

The Ōnin War: History of Its Origins and Background, with a Selective Translation of the Chronicle of Ōnin, by H. Paul Varley 1967.
Chinese Government in Ming Times: Seven Studies, ed. Charles O. Hucker 1969.
The Actors' Analects (Yakusha Rongo), ed. and tr. Charles J. Dunn and Bungō Torigoe 1969.
Self and Society in Ming Thought, by Wm. Theodore de Bary and the Conference on Ming Thought. Also in paperback ed. 1970.
A History of Islamic Philosophy, by Majid Fakhry, 2d ed. 1983.
Phantasies of a Love Thief: The Caurapañatcāśikā Attributed to Bilhaṇa, by Barbara Stoler Miller 1971.
Iqbal: Poet-Philosopher of Pakistan, ed. Hafeez Malik 1971.
The Golden Tradition: An Anthology of Urdu Poetry, ed. and tr. Ahmed Ali. Also in paperback ed. 1973.
Conquerors and Confucians: Aspects of Political Change in Late Yüan China, by John W. Dardess 1973.
The Unfolding of Neo-Confucianism, by Wm. Theodore de Bary and the Conference on Seventeenth-Century Chinese Thought. Also in paperback ed. 1975.
To Acquire Wisdom: The Way of Wang Yang-ming, by Julia Ching 1976.
Gods, Priests, and Warriors: The Bhṛgus of the Mahābhārata, by Robert P. Goldman 1977.
Mei Yao-ch'en and the Development of Early Sung Poetry, by Jonathan Chaves 1976.
The Legend of Semimaru, Blind Musician of Japan, by Susan Matisoff 1977.
Sir Sayyid Ahmad Khan and Muslim Modernization in India and Pakistan, by Hafeez Malik 1980.
The Khilafat Movement: Religious Symbolism and Political Mobilization in India, by Gail Minault 1982.
The World of K'ung Shang-jen: A Man of Letters in Early Ch'ing China, by Richard Strassberg 1983.
The Lotus Boat: The Origins of Chinese Tz'u Poetry in T'ang Popular Culture, by Marsha L. Wagner 1984.
Expressions of Self in Chinese Literature, ed. Robert E. Hegel and Richard C. Hessney 1985.

Songs for the Bride: Women's Voices and Wedding Rites of Rural India, by W. G. Archer; ed. Barbara Stoler Miller and Mildred Archer 1986.

The Confucian Kingship in Korea: Yŏngjo and the Politics of Sagacity, by JaHyun Kim Haboush 1988.

Companions to Asian Studies

Approaches to the Oriental Classics, ed. Wm. Theodore de Bary 1959.

Early Chinese Literature, by Burton Watson. Also in paperback ed. 1962.

Approaches to Asian Civilizations, ed. Wm. Theodore de Bary and Ainslie T. Embree 1964.

The Classic Chinese Novel: A Critical Introduction, by C. T. Hsia. Also in paperback ed. 1968.

Chinese Lyricism: Shih Poetry from the Second to the Twelfth Century, tr. Burton Watson. Also in paperback ed. 1971.

A Syllabus of Indian Civilization, by Leonard A. Gordon and Barbara Stoler Miller 1971.

Twentieth-Century Chinese Stories, ed. C. T. Hsia and Joseph S. M. Lau. Also in paperback ed. 1971.

A Syllabus of Chinese Civilization, by J. Mason Gentzler, 2d ed. 1972.

A Syllabus of Japanese Civilization, by H. Paul Varley, 2d ed. 1972.

An Introduction to Chinese Civilization, ed. John Meskill, with the assistance of J. Mason Gentzler 1973.

An Introduction to Japanese Civilization, ed. Arthur E. Tiedemann 1974.

Ukifune: Love in the Tale of Genji, ed. Andrew Pekarik 1982.

The Pleasures of Japanese Literature, by Donald Keene 1988.

A Guide to Oriental Classics, ed. Wm. Theodore de Bary and Ainslie T. Embree; 3d edition ed. Amy Vladeck Heinrich, 2 vols. 1989.

Introduction to Asian Civilizations

Wm. Theodore de Bary, General Editor

Sources of Japanese Tradition, 1958; paperback ed., 2 vols., 1964. 2d ed., vol. 1, 2001, compiled by Wm. Theodore de Bary, Donald Keene, George

Tanabe, and Paul Varley; vol. 2, 2005, compiled by Wm. Theodore de Bary, Carol Gluck, and Arthur E. Tiedemann; vol. 2, abridged, 2 pts., 2006, compiled by Wm. Theodore de Bary, Carol Gluck, and Arthur E. Tiedemann..

Sources of Indian Tradition, 1958; paperback ed., 2 vols., 1964. 2d ed., 2 vols., 1988.

Sources of Chinese Tradition, 1960, paperback ed., 2 vols., 1964. 2d ed., vol. 1, 1999, compiled by Wm. Theodore de Bary and Irene Bloom; vol. 2, 2000, compiled by Wm. Theodore de Bary and Richard Lufrano.

Sources of Korean Tradition, 1997; 2 vols., vol. 1, 1997, compiled by Peter H. Lee and Wm. Theodore de Bary; vol. 2, 2001, compiled by Yŏngho Ch'oe, Peter H. Lee, and Wm. Theodore de Bary.

Neo-Confucian Studies

Instructions for Practical Living and Other Neo-Confucian Writings by Wang Yang-ming, tr. Wing-tsit Chan 1963.

Reflections on Things at Hand: The Neo-Confucian Anthology, comp. Chu Hsi and Lü Tsu-ch'ien, tr. Wing-tsit Chan 1967.

Self and Society in Ming Thought, by Wm. Theodore de Bary and the Conference on Ming Thought. Also in paperback ed. 1970.

The Unfolding of Neo-Confucianism, by Wm. Theodore de Bary and the Conference on Seventeenth-Century Chinese Thought. Also in paperback ed. 1975.

Principle and Practicality: Essays in Neo-Confucianism and Practical Learning, ed. Wm. Theodore de Bary and Irene Bloom. Also in paperback ed. 1979.

The Syncretic Religion of Lin Chao-en, by Judith A. Berling 1980.

The Renewal of Buddhism in China: Chu-hung and the Late Ming Synthesis, by Chün-fang Yü 1981.

Neo-Confucian Orthodoxy and the Learning of the Mind-and-Heart, by Wm. Theodore de Bary 1981.

Yüan Thought: Chinese Thought and Religion Under the Mongols, ed. Hok-lam Chan and Wm. Theodore de Bary 1982.

The Liberal Tradition in China, by Wm. Theodore de Bary 1983.

The Development and Decline of Chinese Cosmology, by John B. Henderson 1984.

The Rise of Neo-Confucianism in Korea, by Wm. Theodore de Bary and Ja-Hyun Kim Haboush 1985.

Chiao Hung and the Restructuring of Neo-Confucianism in Late Ming, by Edward T. Ch'ien 1985.

Neo-Confucian Terms Explained: Pei-hsi tzu-i, by Ch'en Ch'un, ed. and tr. Wing-tsit Chan 1986.

Knowledge Painfully Acquired: K'un-chih chi, by Lo Ch'in-shun, ed. and tr. Irene Bloom 1987.

To Become a Sage: The Ten Diagrams on Sage Learning, by Yi T'oegye, ed. and tr. Michael C. Kalton 1988.

The Message of the Mind in Neo-Confucian Thought, by Wm. Theodore de Bary 1989.

The Columbia Anthology of Modern Chinese Literature, 2d ed., ed. Joseph S. M. Lau and Howard Goldblatt.